Ptsd

A Comprehensive Guide to Managing Ptsd

(Compassionate Strategies to Begin Healing From Childhood Trauma)

Steve Ridenour

Published By **Oliver Leish**

Steve Ridenour

Ptsd: A Comprehensive Guide to Managing Ptsd (Compassionate Strategies to Begin Healing From Childhood Trauma)

ISBN   978-1-7776381-8-4

Legal & Disclaimer

The information contained in this book is not designed to replace or take the place of any form of medicine or professional medical advice. The information in this book has been provided for educational & entertainment purposes only.

The information contained in this book has been compiled from sources deemed reliable, and it is accurate to the best of the Author's knowledge; however, the Author cannot guarantee its accuracy and validity and cannot be held liable for any errors or omissions. Changes are periodically made to this book. You must consult your doctor or get professional medical advice before using any of the suggested remedies, techniques, or information in this book.

Table Of Contents

Chapter 1: Understanding Ptsd

Post-Traumatic Stress Disorder (PTSD) is a mental health disorder that is complex which can manifest in people who have been through or witness an event that was traumatic. The chapter discusses the basic aspects of the understanding of PTSD and the effects on trauma, its symptoms and diagnoses, as well as the prevalence as well as statistics pertaining to this disorder.

The Impact of Trauma

Trauma is a traumatic situation that threatens an individual's physical and psychological health. This can result from natural disasters as well as combat exposure, accidents or even the threat of violence. In the event of trauma the body and brain react in a variety of ways. The effects of trauma may be far more than the original moment. In some people, it may lead to the development of PTSD.

Symptoms and Diagnosis

The symptoms of PTSD include various signs that could significantly affect people's lives. They are typically classified into four groups: disturbing ideas and memories, avoiding behaviours as well as negative mood swings and cognition, as well changes in arousal and reaction. Patients suffering from PTSD might experience flashbacks, nightmares and avoidance of triggers emotions numbness, hyperarousal and problems with concentration as well as sleeping.

Finding out if you have PTSD requires a thorough evaluation conducted by qualified medical professionals. Clinicians use accepted diagnostic guidelines, like those within the Diagnostic and Statistical Manual of Mental Disorders (DSM-5),

PTSD Symptom Checklist

1. Intrusion Symptoms:

Recurrent distressing thoughts or nightmares relating to the traumatizing event.

Intense or long-lasting emotional distress after being exposed to the thoughts of the trauma.

Dissociative or flashback reactions that make people feel like they are experiencing the same trauma in a different way.

2. Avoidance Symptoms:

Avoidance or attempts to avoid painful thoughts, emotions, memories or reminders that are associated with the traumatizing event.

Averting situations, actions and people who could cause memories or recollections of the painful experience.

Participation or interest has decreased of significant events.

3. Negative Alterations in Cognition and Mood Symptoms:

Persistent negative belief or beliefs about oneself, others or the world.

The negative emotional states are anxiety, fear or guilt. or detachment.

Less interest in sports which were once enjoyed.

Feeling isolated or disengaged with others.

4. Alterations in Arousal and Reactivity Symptoms:

Irritable behavior or angry eruptions, or aggressive behaviors.

Self-destructive or reckless conduct.

Hypervigilance or always being looking for threat.

The exaggerated response to startle.

Troubles with concentration, or sleep problems.

5. Duration of Symptoms:

Check the length of symptoms and determine the duration of their persistence (e.g. lesser than one month, 1-3 months, 3-6 month, 6-months, or even longer).

6. Functional Impairment:

Examine the effects of the symptoms on different aspects of function, like schools or at work and social interactions, as well as relationships as well as daily tasks.

It's important to know that PCL-5 is a standardized evaluation instrument that includes specific tests and responses to assess the extent of PTSD symptoms.

Prevalence and Statistics

The condition can be affecting people of all ages, genders and backgrounds. It is essential to comprehend the severity and prevalence of the disorder in order to understand its importance and effect on the society. Research has shown that around 7 -8% of the population is likely to experience PTSD at one point or another. Particularly among certain groups like veterans of the military and survivors of sexual assault, incidence rates could be greater.

Statistics also emphasize the necessity of dealing with and knowing about PTSD. There is evidence that suggests females are much more likely be affected by PTSD as compared to men. Additionally, those with a history of past experiences with mental illness or trauma could be at higher chance of developing. It's important to understand that PTSD isn't restricted to particular demographics, and can impact all who have experienced an event that was traumatic.

Chapter 2: Foundations Of Cognitive Processing Therapy

Cognitive Processing Therapy (CPT) is widely recognized as an successful treatment option for people suffering from post-traumatic stress disorder (PTSD). This chapter offers an outline of basic concepts, benefits as well as techniques that are related to CPT.

An Overview of CPT

Cognitive Processing Therapy a proven psychotherapy which focuses on the traumatic memories that are the source of PTSD. The primary goal of CPT is helping individuals to adapt and sort through their beliefs and thoughts regarding the traumatic experience. In doing this, CPT aims to alleviate discomforting symptoms and boost the overall health of individuals.

CPT works on the premise that when people experience emotional trauma, their views of security, trust and self-worth are impacted. By retraining their cognitive processes, CPT helps individuals challenge and change their thinking patterns with more rational and balanced beliefs. Through developing a better perception of the trauma as well as its aftermath, patients are able to experience less ailment and better health.

Benefits and Effectiveness

CPT is extensively studied and has always provided solid results in treatment of PTSD. Many studies have shown substantial decreases in PTSD symptoms, as well as improvement for co-occurring illnesses like anxiety and depression.

One of the main positive aspects of CPT is the focus on helping individuals become empowered by equipping people with the necessary skills and resources to test and alter their thinking methods. It allows people to gain control over and be in charge of their lives. This results in greater self-confidence as well as improved mental health.

Additionally, CPT has lasting effects even after treatment is completed. People who undergo

CPT frequently report constant improvement in symptoms, indicating that the knowledge gained during treatment are useful and applicable in the long run.

Principles and Techniques

Cognitive Processing Therapy can be supported by a set of core values that guide the therapeutic process. This includes collaboration between the therapist and client in identifying and reviewing the underlying beliefs and thoughts that are not adaptive while encouraging active engagement as well as participation in therapy.

CPT uses a range of methods to meet its therapeutic objectives. One of the most common strategies that is used is Socratic asking, in which the therapist is able to engage the client with critical thinking and inquiry. By asking open-ended questions therapy, the therapist assists the client to confront and redefine the negative and distorted thought pattern.

A different method employed as part of CPT involves the use of writing accounts. The idea is to have people record detailed descriptions about their experiences that were traumatic. Writing can help people organize their feelings and thoughts with a controlled, structured way, which helps in the healing process and solving concerns arising from the experience.

In addition, CPT incorporates cognitive-behavioral therapy (CBT) methods including relaxation techniques as well as breathing exercises and behavior experiments to improve emotional control and improve coping abilities.

Dispelling common misconceptions regarding CPT

The misperceptions about Cognitive Processing Therapy can hinder the effectiveness and implementation of this therapy. Recognizing and removing these myths is crucial to make sure that people benefit from this effective therapy approach.

A common myth is that CPT is simply "thinking positive" or dismissing the trauma's effects. Actually, CPT acknowledges the complexity and repercussions of trauma and provides a safe place for people to face and deal with their feelings. Another myth is that CPT ignores trauma victims their unique culture and personal circumstances. In fact, CPT encourages cultural sensitivity and adaptation in order to ensure that the process of therapy respects and is in line with the clients' convictions, values, and the cultural context.

Chapter 3: Assessment And Evaluation

Evaluation and assessment are essential to the successful therapy of PTSD. The chapter discusses the diverse aspects of measuring and evaluating PTSD and includes the screening process for PTSD as well as testing diagnostic criteria, and evaluating the severity of symptoms. Knowing these assessment techniques is vital for an accurate diagnosis as well as appropriate treatment strategies.

Screening for PTSD

The screening process for PTSD is the first step to identify individuals who might suffer from symptoms that suggest PTSD. Screening instruments are made to offer a preliminari indicator of the possibility of PTSD and assist in identifying individuals who require further assessment. The most commonly used screening tools for PTSD comprise those on the PTSD Checklist to DSM-5 (PCL-5) as well as the Impact of Event Scale (IES).

It is crucial to understand the fact that screening tools are not diagnostic instruments on their own they are merely an initial phase in the process of assessing. If a positive screening outcome indicates that there is a need to further evaluate by using valid diagnosis methods.

Diagnostic Criteria Evaluation

Evaluation of diagnostic criteria is an extensive assessment by mental health specialists. This document, the Diagnostic and Statistical Manual of Mental Disorders (DSM-5) is an established set of guidelines for diagnosing PTSD. The criteria for diagnosis include signs, durations, and functional impairments that must be evident for a PTSD diagnosis.

In the course of evaluating during the evaluation, doctors collect data about the traumatized person's events, their time and intensity of the symptoms, as well as their effect on the daily routine. A thorough evaluation allows professionals to assess whether the requirements for diagnosing

PTSD meet and whether additional conditions need to be assessed or excluded.

Assessing Symptom Severity

Analyzing the intensity of PTSD symptoms aids in understanding the effects of the disorder on the lives of individuals and helps in planning treatment. Several standardized measures are available to assess symptom severity, such as the Clinician-Administered PTSD Scale (CAPS-5) and the PTSD Symptom Scale Interview (PSSI).

The assessment tools provide a systematic and well-organized approach for assessing the intensity and frequency of PTSD symptoms. Knowing the severity of symptoms aids clinicians in choosing the best treatment strategy as well as monitoring the progress made during the treatment process, and in evaluating results.

Chapter 4: Psycho Education For Trauma

Psycho education is a key factor in the treatment of post-traumatic stress disorder (PTSD). The chapter contains accurate data and information about PTSD and includes a thorough understanding of the neurobiology behind trauma, informing individuals as well as their families, and removing the stigma associated with PTSD.

Understanding the Neurobiology of Trauma

Informing people about the neurobiology that is involved in trauma will help to understand how the traumatic events affect the brain as well as the body. The knowledge gained can assist those with PTSD to understand their experiences and help them reduce the guilt or shame that comes with trauma.

The concept of the system of stress, which includes the fight or flight response helps people comprehend what triggers them to experience increased alertness, hypervigilance and other physical symptoms. It is essential to remember the fact that these are typical responses to a stressful or traumatic incident.

Informing people about the effects of trauma on their brain particularly the amygdala the hippocampus and prefrontal cortex could provide valuable insights on memory processing, emotional regulation, as well as cognitive functions. Learning about the neurobiological components that trauma has can help develop an underlying sense of confidence and normalization, which can reduce self-judgment as well as increasing self-compassion.

Education for Individuals and Their Support Systems

Offering psychoeducation regarding PTSD to people and their family members is vital in fostering empathy, understanding and efficient assistance. The education helps individuals deal with their PTSD issues better and assists loved ones in providing adequate assistance.

Training for those suffering from PTSD must include information on typical symptoms like disturbing thoughts, avoidance behaviours and excessive arousal. In describing the impact these issues on the daily routine and interpersonal relationships could help people create strategies to overcome difficulties and enhance their overall well-being.

Instructing people to practice self-care like relaxation exercises meditation, mindfulness exercises, as well as effective coping methods, will help them participate actively in their journey to recovery. Psychoeducation could also contain the availability of resources including support groups, as well as counseling options that encourage those seeking help to get it.

To support networks, which include parents, family members, and professional professionals, education on the nature of PTSD is a great way to help build empathy and awareness. The knowledge gained can assist them to understand the importance of providing an environment that is supportive and not judgmental that validates the experience of those suffering from PTSD and also avoid triggering triggers and the re-traumatization process.

Breaking the Stigma Surrounding PTSD

Psychoeducation regarding PTSD can play a significant part in breaking down the stigma attached to this disorder. A lot of people suffering from PTSD suffer from social stigmas or isolation as well as misconceptions. The power of education can help combat these stereotypes by providing accurate information, and creating awareness for the community.

The sharing of stories of resilience and healing can help humanize the suffering of those with the condition and show the importance of seeking assistance as an act of courage. The education initiatives may include the public in awareness programs, community events, as well as media campaigns that challenge the stereotypes of society and encourage the understanding of.

Making safe places for honest discussion and to promote the importance of mental health education can to reduce the stigma and isolation that are often connected with PTSD. A sense that is supportive and accepting can be created through engaging in discussions about mental health, and by challenging the myths.

Setting Realistic Treatment Goals

Collaboration in setting treatment goals that are realistic is an essential aspect in making preparations the client for Cognitive Processing Therapy. Clients and clinicians are able to work together in identifying the outcomes they wish to see and then establish precise, quantifiable, realizable pertinent, time-bound (SMART) objectives. Set goals that are realistic will help create an understanding of direction and goal-setting, which instills confidence and optimism in the patient. This also facilitates understanding among the participants of the outcomes desired, and helps align both the clinician and client with respect to their goals for the therapeutic goals.

Chapter 5: Cognitive Restructuring

Cognitive restructuring is a key element of cognitive-behavioral therapy (CBT) along with other approaches to treating diverse mental health disorders such as post-traumatic stress disorder (PTSD). This chapter concentrates on cognitive restructuring. It includes finding maladaptive or negative thinking patterns and cognitive distortions and replacing harmful beliefs with more constructive ones.

Identifying Negative and Maladaptive Thoughts

The first step of mental restructuring is to recognize harmful and unadaptive thinking patterns which cause distress and increase the manifestations of PTSD. The thoughts are usually self-blame and blame, as well as negative predications as well as catastrophic thoughts and generalization. They may be automatic and unconscious, causing negativity and negative behaviors.

By monitoring their own self and becoming aware, individuals are able to spot the negative thoughts that happen. Methods like thought journals or journals may be utilized to track and analyze the thoughts. In observing their thought patterns, individuals will be able to understand the processes of their brain that cause the symptoms they experience.

Thought Record: Challenging Negative Thoughts

Step 1: Identify the Situation

Think about a recent incident or incident that caused you to feel anger or sadness. Record a concise account of the event and include any particular details of the event, who was involved and the feelings you felt.

Situation: For example Situation: You receive a contact from a relative inviting you to attend a party however, you decided to decline because of anxiety and fear of crowds.

_____

_____

_____

Step 2: Describe Emotions

Find out the emotions you experienced when you were in that situation. As precise as you can and then rate the intensity of each emotion using an 0-to-10 scale, which is 0 representing no intensity and 10 being intense level of intensity.

Emotions: Example: Anxiety (8/10), Fear (7/10), Disappointment (6/10)

_____
_____

Step 3: Identify Automatic Thoughts

Note the thoughts and automatic thought patterns that ran through your mind in the course of your situation. They are instantaneous, automatic and sometimes negative thoughts add to the stress. You should try to get the basic idea of your thoughts, without judgement or evaluation.

Automatic Thoughts: Examples: "I can't handle crowded places anymore." "Everyone will judge me and think I'm weak for avoiding social gatherings."

_____

_____

_____

_____

_____

_____

_____

_____

Step 4: Challenge Negative Thoughts

Then, look at the evidence against and for every automatic thought. You can ask yourself these questions to question the legitimacy of your negative thinking:

Do you have any evidence to is in support of this idea?

_____

_____

_____

Do you have evidence that is in opposition to this assertion?

_____

_____

_____

_____

Did I have similar thoughts before How exact did they prove to be?

_____

_____

_____

_____

Are I just assuming the most likely scenario and not considering alternatives?

_____

_____

_____

_____

How might someone else who has a good relationship with me think about this?

_____

_____

_____

_____

Challenging Negative Thoughts:

First thought: "I can't handle crowded places anymore."

There is no evidence that supports this assertion The evidence is not there.

The evidence is not in support of this assertion The fact is that I've attended many massive events and not experienced severe anxiety. I've learned and applied techniques to cope with anxiety.

Second thought "Everyone will judge me and think I'm weak for avoiding social gatherings."

The evidence to support this belief There is no evidence to support this belief.

The evidence isn't in support of this assertion Friends have been supportive and understanding at times, whenever I've spoken about my anxiety. They have been aware of my issues and haven't criticised me in any way.

Step 5: Generate Balanced Thoughts

Based on the information you've collected Based on your evidence, develop more balanced and real-world alternatives to challenge the negative initial thinking.

_____

_____

_____

_____

_____

_____

_____

_____

_____

Balanced Thoughts:

1. Thought: "I have managed crowded places before, and I can handle this situation with my coping skills too."

Second thought "My friends have shown understanding and support in the past and are aware of my struggles. They are unlikely to judge me negatively."

Step 6: Re-evaluate Emotions

Re-rate the strength of your feelings after weighing the rational thoughts. Be aware of any changes in the strength of your feelings and note them down below.

The emotions that follow challenging thoughts are For example anxiety (5/10) (five/10), Fear (4/10) and Disappointment (3/10)

_____

_____

Step 7: Action Plan

With the balanced perspective you have weighed, determine a sensible decision you will take as a reaction to the circumstances. Make a detailed strategy that is aligned to your fresh perspective.

Action Plan Example: Take the next invitation to attend a social event and develop coping strategies like meditation and self-talk to help manage anxiety.

_____

_____

_____

_____

_____

_____

Cognitive Reframing Exercise: Changing Negative Perspectives

Step 1: Identify the Negative Thought

Find a negative idea or belief regarding the PTSD trauma or triggers. Write down the idea which you would like to transform in a way that captures the essence of it.

Negative Thoughts: Examples: "My past experiences permanently damage me, and I will never be able to lead a fulfilling life."

_____

_____

_____

_____

Step 2: Recognize the Emotional Impact

Recognize the feelings that come up as you accept the negative thoughts. Think about the effect it has on your wellbeing and its limitations upon your life.

Emotional Impact Example feeling defeated, hopeless and disenchanted from working towards your goals in life and with connections.

_____

_____

_____

_____

Step 3: Question the Negative Thought

Refuse to believe in negative thoughts by asking yourself a set of questions to stimulate an open mind and exploration of different viewpoints. Be sure to answer each question truthfully and with a thoughtful approach.

Questioning the Negative Thought:

Does anyone have evidence that is in support of this belief?

Examples: Though my recent challenges have been a bit difficult However, I have also experienced times of improvement, strength and growth.

_____

_____

_____

_____

Do you have evidence that is in opposition to this belief?

Examples: I've seen individuals who had been through similar traumas, overcame their challenges and live life that is full of happiness. This indicates that growth and healing are feasible.

_____

_____

_____

_____

What suggestions would you give an acquaintance who has the negative belief?

Example: If a person I know was in my position I would advise them to look at the accomplishments they've made. They should focus on their strengths and look for support in order to help facilitate recovery and personal development.

_____

_____

_____

_____

Step 4: Generate a Balanced Reframe

Based on your answers to the questions phase Develop a balanced, real-world alternative which challenges your negative beliefs.

The Balanced Reframe example: "While my past experiences have been challenging, they have also shaped me positively. I am resilient, compassionate, and capable of healing and leading a fulfilling life."

_____

_____

_____

_____

Step 5: Embrace the New Perspective

Rethink the rationale and think about what ways this change in viewpoint can benefit your lifestyle. Think about the possibilities and potential opportunities you can unlock by embracing this new conviction.

Accepting the New Perspective For example: by recognizing my strength and resilience I'm able to tackle the challenges with confidence, and look for new opportunities to grow. A new mindset lets me envision the future with purpose as well as purpose and joy.

Decatastrophizing Exercise: Challenging Catastrophic Thinking

Step 1: Identify the Catastrophic Thought

Find a particular catastrophic thought or belief that is related to the triggers for your PTSD or any traumatic memories. Write down the idea you wish to deathastrophize making sure that you have captured its essence.

Catastrophic Thinking: For example: "If I encounter a trigger, I will completely lose control and panic, embarrassing myself in front of others."

_____

_____

_____

_____

Step 2: Recognize the Emotional Impact

Recognize the feelings that come up whenever you are enslaved by the thought of a catastrophic event. Think about the effect it has on your wellbeing and the limits it places upon your life.

Emotional Impact Example Arousing anxiety, a sense of worry, and a massive need to stay away from circumstances that could result in these disastrous results.

_____

_____

_____

_____

Step 3: Challenge the Catastrophic Thought

Refuse to believe in the apocalyptic by asking yourself a set of questions to encourage inquiry and an exploration of alternatives. Respond to each question with honesty and with a lot of thought.

Questioning the Catastrophic Thought:

What evidence can be found to support the apocalyptic consequence?

Example: Although I've had a few unpleasant symptoms in the past, it's not a given that each cause will trigger an outright disorientation and embarrassing.

_____

_____

_____

_____

Do you have any other possible explanations?

An example: It's possible to use strategies for coping, like the practice of deep breathing or grounding in order to control my anxiety, and avoid an attack of panic. I've successfully employed these techniques previously.

_____

_____

_____

_____

Did I have success navigating similar scenarios previously?

Examples: I have had occasions when I faced emotional triggers, and dealt with them with moderate calm. These examples show how I manage my feelings and react effectively.

_____

_____

_____

_____

What is the likelihood of this devastating scenario compared with more feasible scenarios?

An example: Even though I could feel anxious but it's more sensible to imagine that I am able to utilize my coping methods to seek help, as well as deal with the issue without losing control.

_____

_____

_____

_____

Step 4: Generate a Balanced Perspective

Based on the responses you give to the questions Develop a balanced, reality-based perspective that challenges terrifying notion.

A Balanced View: An example: "Encountering triggers does not automatically mean I will completely lose control. I have coping skills that can help me manage my anxiety, and I can reach out for support if needed. I can face triggers with resilience and composure."

_____

_____

_____

Step 5: Embrace the Balanced Perspective

Take a look at the balanced view and think about how this outlook will positively affect your reactions to triggers, and your overall health. Think about how you can respond in a calm and efficient manner to stressful circumstances.

Accepting the Balanced View: Examples: If I adopt this perspective of balance I am able to approach triggers with more confidence and lessen the influence they exert over me. I'm able to respond in a way that is adaptive and keep my cool and improve my feeling of control and wellbeing.

_____
_____
_____
_____
_____
_____

Cognitive Distancing Exercise: Creating Mental Space

Step 1: Find a Quiet and Comfortable Space

Find a peaceful and quiet area to perform the practice without interruptions. It is advisable to take a moment to relax into a calm position, and pay attention to the breath.

Step 2: Close Your Eyes and Visualize

Relax your eyes and imagine those thoughts or images that you wish to get away from.

The image or the thought to get into your head with no judgement.

Step 3: Observe the Distressing Thought

When you imagine the troubling idea or memory, try to imagine it's separate from the person you are. Imagine it as a moving cloud, or a film playing on screen, or another image that allows you to see it as distinct from the core of your persona.

Step 4: Create Distance

Imagine walking away from a traumatic idea or thought, creating space between yourself and the thought or image. Imagine yourself walking onto a balcony that overlooks the scene, or sitting away from the screen of a movie.

5. Observe the scene the subject with curiosity

With this vantage point take a look at the troubling thoughts or memories in awe and detachedness. Instead of being caught with the emotion or specifics, look at it as though you were an objective observer.

Step 6: Notice Your Reactions

Take note of your physical and emotional responses which arise when you look at your distressing memory or thought at an in-between distant distance. Pay attention to how your mood and physical sensations alter when you try to separate yourself mentally from the idea.

Step 7: Remind Yourself of the Separation

If you feel emotionally involved or stressed, remind yourself that you're independent of the thoughts or the memory. Instill the belief that you've created space and are able to observe the space without becoming distracted.

Step 8: Practice Self-Compassion

When you perform this activity, you should be considerate and gentle with yourself. Moving away from thoughts that are causing you distress isn't easy to master, and acquiring this ability requires time and effort.

Step 9: Return to the Present Moment

If you are able to observe the troubling image or thought at a distance, gradually restore your focus to the present. Inhale deeply and then open your eyes and regain your connection with your surroundings.

Mindfulness-Based Cognitive Therapy Exercise: Cultivating Present-Moment Awareness

Step 1: Find a Quiet and Comfortable Space

Choose a calm and relaxing area to perform the exercise with no interruptions. Spend a few minutes to relax into a calm position and pay focus to the present.

Chapter 6: Processing Traumatic Memories

Processing traumatic experiences is an essential part of the therapy process for those suffering from post-traumatic stress disorder (PTSD). This chapter examines a variety of methods of emotional processing, such as the use of narratives and the imaginal approach. The chapter also focuses on the importance in externalizing and transformating traumatizing experiences in the therapeutic process.

Techniques for Emotional Processing

The process of emotional processing is the act of actively being in touch with and observing the feelings associated with painful memories. The process helps people deal with and resolve the emotions that are troubling them, while reducing their frequency and intensity.

The most popular method for emotional processing is called exposure therapy. The process gradually exposes people to memories, thoughts as well as the situations that are associated with the event that caused them to be traumatized safely and in a controlled method. When confronted repeatedly with these traumatic stimulus, people can reduce their emotions and gain an understanding of how to master the traumatizing memories.

Narrative Exposure and Imaginal Exposure

Narrative Exposure Therapy (NET) is a scientifically-based procedure that helps patients process and integrate traumatizing memories through the creation of the narrative that reflects their experience. With a structured and supportive method, patients are instructed to describe their experiences in a precise and sequential way. The therapist assists the person to write down their emotions as well as thoughts about the trauma. This helps with process of organizing and making meaning from the experiences.

The process of imaginal exposure, on contrary, is the process of mentally replaying the event in guided images. It allows people to visualize vividly the specifics of their traumatic event along with the emotions that accompany it and the associated sensory experiences. In the process of repeatedly engaging in imaginative exposure, people can slowly manage and reduce the emotional impact caused by painful memories.

Externalizing and Transforming Traumatic Experiences

Externalizing trauma can be a healing method that allows people to view the experience of trauma as distinct from the person they are. This method allows people to get away from the overwhelming thoughts and thoughts that are associated with the experience. It allows individuals to develop a fresh view and open up the psychological space needed for healing.

Transformation of traumatic events involves shifting out of a sense of victimization towards a feeling of resiliency and improvement. This is a process of revising personal narratives, and looking at positive elements that emerged because of the trauma. This involves acknowledging and recognizing your strengths, and creating an awareness of the post-traumatic process as a way to grow.

Therapists can employ psychological restructuring techniques as well as positive psychology intervention and exercises for making meaning to aid the process of change. Through helping people rethink their meanings associated with their experiences that have caused trauma Therapists aid in their capacity to discover meaning, motivation, and progress when faced with adversity.

Chapter 7: Exposure Therapy

Exposure therapy is an extensively practiced and scientifically-proven treatment for post-traumatic stress disorders (PTSD) and various anxiety conditions. This chapter will focus on the methods and principles of exposure therapy. This includes the gradual exposure to trauma-related stimuli in a systematic manner, desensitization techniques, as well as the emergence in virtual reality therapies as a method for exposure.

Gradual Exposure to Trauma-related Stimuli

Exposure therapy involves subjecting individuals to stimuli that are related to trauma through a systematic and controlled way, which allows individuals to face their anxieties and fears. Exposure therapy can be carried out differently, based upon the patient's personal comfort levels as well as the therapeutic objectives.

When it comes to PTSD it is possible to gradually expose be obtained through the imaginal process or through real-life exposure. Imagined exposure is a process that involves the use of guided imagery. It is where people are able to mentally revisit the trauma by describing the event in details and expressing their feelings. In real-world exposure, you have to confront the triggers or situations that are associated with the trauma with a controlled and gradual method.

Systematic Desensitization

The technique of systematic desensitization employed in the field of exposure therapy that helps people slowly reduce anxiety and fears in response in response to stimuli triggered by trauma. This process combines techniques for relaxation, like deep breathing or gradual muscles relaxation, along with the idea of or imagining the stimuli that trigger fear.

When people are exposed to the stimuli they fear when they engage in relaxation exercises and relaxation techniques, they slowly learn to connect the stimulus with calm instead of intense fear. This can help to alter the person's fear-based conditioned response, and create an adaptive and more well-controlled response to the trauma-related stimuli.

Virtual Reality Therapy for Exposure

Virtual real-world (VR) therapy has become a cutting-edge and widely used tool for exposure therapy. The process involves creating a simulation setting that is reminiscent of real-world situations that are related to the trauma. By using the use of a virtual reality headset users can be immersed in the safety of a safe, controlled environment that allows them to experience the trauma-related triggers.

Virtual reality therapy has an advantage that is unique in offering a full-immersive and authentic experience, which increases the efficacy of the therapy. This allows patients to get the sensation of being in the virtual environment, which can make the experience more vibrant and memorable.

It is useful for those who be unable to access actual exposure or experiences which are hard to replicate within traditional therapeutic environments. Virtual reality therapy offers the security and control needed to gradually expose, which reduces the possibility of traumatizing recurrence while giving people the opportunity to face and deal with their traumatizing memories.

How to Practice Exposure Therapy

Exposure therapy is often utilized to treat anxiety-related problems and fears. It helps reduce anxiety and fear by slowly exposing people to their fearful object or circumstance. This is a thorough exercise on the best ways to use exposure therapy.

1. Find the Fear: Determine your specific fear-inducing scenario that you wish to address. It can be anything that is a particular phobia (e.g. the fear of the heights) or social anxiety (e.g. fears of speaking in public).

_____

_____

2. Make the fear Hierarchy Write down an inventory of the situations that are related to your fear. They should be listed with the least anxiety-inducing. As an example, if are afraid of spiders, your hierarchy may include looking at photos of spiders. Then, you could be within the same space as spiders, and then being able to touch the spider.

_____

_____

_____

_____

3. Relaxation Methods: Prior to starting exposure, try relaxing methods like deep breathing exercises, gradual muscles relaxation or even mindfulness. These methods can assist you to control anxiety while exposed.

4. Experimentation Steps: Begin by exposing yourself to the situation that is least stressful

in your organization. As you progress, make yourself vulnerable to your most feared circumstance while maintaining your calm level. The following steps will guide you through every exposure:

a. Create a goal: Set an objective during each session of exposure for you to achieve the fear. This could include being in the same situation for a certain amount of time or engaging in an task related to the fear.

b. Experiment: Step into the scenario or confront the fearful object. You can continue to use breathing techniques that help manage anxiety. Keep the scene until the anxiety diminishes (habituation).

C. Note your anxiety level You can use a scale ranging from 1-10 to evaluate your anxiety levels prior to as well as following exposure. This will help you track the progress you make in time, as anxiety reduces.

D. Repeat the exercise and then gradually advance Do the exercise often, slowly climbing through the fear hierarchy making yourself vulnerable to scenarios which trigger higher levels of anxiety.

5. Find Support: You may want to consider practicing exposure therapy in conjunction with a licensed therapy therapist who has experience using this method. They can offer guidance and assistance, as well as provide a secure and safe therapy experience.

Keep in mind that exposure therapy can be difficult, but it is intended to aid you to get over your fear gradually. You must approach every session with the intention of facing your fears. You must also remain patient through the entire process.

Chapter 8: Managing Anxiety And Panic

Controlling anxieties and fears is a crucial element of treating people who suffer from anxiety disorders. This includes Post-traumatic Stress Disorder (PTSD). This chapter is focused on how to deal with panic and anxiety, which includes cognitive strategies to cope such as relaxation techniques, dealing with behaviors of avoidance, and much other.

Cognitive Coping Strategies

Cognitive coping strategies are designed to influence and change negative thoughts that lead to panic and anxiety. The individual can lessen the amount and frequency of anxiety by acknowledging and removing unhelpful thought patterns.

A common strategy for coping with cognitive stress is to use cognitive restructuring. This method is about finding and evaluating the validity of anxiety-related thoughts. People learn to question their negative thoughts and then replace them with rational and more realistic thoughts. The individual can control their emotions and decrease anxiety by reframe negative self-doubt as well as catastrophic thinking.

A different effective strategy for coping with cognitive stress is to stop thinking. It involves conscious recognition the anxiety and interrupting it through the mental act of using the word "stop" or physically snapping with a rubber band to the wrist. In this way, by breaking the thought pattern it is possible to break up the anxious cycle and shift their attention to positive ideas.

Relaxation Techniques and Breathing Exercises

Breathing exercises and relaxation techniques can be beneficial in dealing with panic attacks and anxiety. They help the person to activate the body's relaxation reaction as well as reduce the physiological signs related to anxiety.

Exercises that involve deep breathing like diaphragmatic and breath paced, involves breathing slowly and deeply. The breathing technique triggers your body's relaxation response which reduces heart rate and helps to create a feeling of tranquility. Through regular practice of deep breathing people can improve the ability of their body to deal with anxiety and stress.

The process of progressive muscle relaxation can be an additional efficient method. It involves stretching and relaxing different muscles throughout the body. This helps promote relaxation in the body and decreasing tension in the muscles that can be caused by anxiety. Through systematically relaxing the body, people can improve their general feeling of calm and ease the effects of stress.

Deep Breathing for Relaxation and Grounding

In the course of CPT, or Cognitive Processing Therapy (CPT) for PTSD It is crucial to include relaxation methods to help regulate emotions as well as grounding. Breathing deeply is a straightforward but effective technique that will assist in relaxing the nervous system as well as promote calmness. Through this practice, we can guide you through a long-distance breathing routine that you can utilize to lessen anxiety and get more calm.

1. Find a peaceful and comfy spot to lie or sit down. You should ensure that you don't get distracted during the workout.

2. Keep your eyes closed or just a little open, which ever is more relaxing for you.

3. Start by paying awareness to your breathing. Pay attention to your breathing, without attempting to alter anything.

4. Take a slow, deeply breathe through your nostrils. While you breath, think of the lungs being filled with an energizing, soothing breath.

5. Inhale and continue to breathe and exhale, keep a count of 4 within your head, and allow your breath to become smooth and constant.

6. When you've reached maximum inhale level, stop for a few seconds and hold your breath in a relaxed manner.

7. Then, exhale slowly and deeply by mouth, dissolving stress or anxiety through each exhale.

8. When you exhale and exhale, begin counting to four within your head, keeping the same steady and smooth beat.

9. Continue this breathing exercise throughout the day, keeping your attention on the feeling of your breath coming into and going out of your body.

10. When you continue to take deep breaths, be aware of any discomfort or tension within your body. As you breathe, think of relaxing and releasing the areas of tension.

11. When your mind starts to wander, or thoughts that are distracting come to mind, simply draw your attention back to your breath and use the breath as a anchor for your current moment.

12. Keep this up for five to ten minutes, or whatever time feels right to you.

13. If you're ready to end the workout, you can take a few more slow breaths. Allow you to fully experience the feeling of relaxation and grounding completely.

14. Take a moment to open your eyes and observe for a few seconds what you are feeling, then slowly return to your normal activities.

Keep in mind that breathing deeply is useful when you're feeling stressed and anxious or feel disconnected. Try this routinely, as time passes, you might notice a greater feeling of peace and a better wellbeing.

Progressive Muscle Relaxation for Tension Release and Calming

When it comes to Cognitive Processing Therapy (CPT) to treat PTSD It is essential to include relaxation methods which help ease tension and create a feeling of peace. The Progressive muscle Relaxation (PMR) can be an example of a technique that is able to help reduce the tension of muscles across the body. People can feel more relaxed when they learn to detect the tension in their muscles and then release it. This workout will lead you through a progressive muscle Relaxation technique that can be used to reduce stress in the context of your CPT experience.

1. Find a peaceful and comfy location to lay or sit down. Be sure that you don't get interrupted during the workout.

2. Be sure to keep your eyes open, based upon your preferences.

3. Begin by taking several deep breaths. Breathe slowly, breathing in then exhaling any tension or stress that you feel with every breath.

4. Start by putting your feet on the floor. Engage the muscles of your feet. Do this by curving your toes down, retaining the tension for just a few seconds before letting go of the

tension completely and feeling the subsequent relaxation. Pay attention to the differences between relaxation and tension.

5. Slowly work up your calves. Bring your feet toward your face, then tighten your muscles around your calves. Then, keep the tension in place for a couple of seconds before relaxing completely and being relaxed as you go.

6. Then, you can move towards your the thighs. The muscles of your thighs, as if you press them against the floor which you're lying on or sitting on. Tension should be held, and after that relax, and feel the relaxing sensation.

7. Keep moving towards your buttocks and the pelvic region. Intensify your muscles to this area, and let them go and feel the relaxation feeling that will spread throughout this region.

8. Move your abdominal muscles to the side. Intensify your abdominal muscles by pushing them backwards, and after which you can let

the tension go by allowing the muscles to relax completely.

9. Make sure you are moving your chest, and lower return. Take a deep breath. Expand your chest while taking in air. Take the breath, and hold the tension. Exhale gradually, taking out the tension and air fully. Relax your chest and fall into a comfortable position.

10. Concentrate on your shoulders. Move them toward your ears. Tense the muscles. Then allow them to drop abruptly to let go of any tightness that remains.

11. Begin to move your arms and hands. Hold your hands tightly and tighten them and feel the tension build up throughout your forearms, hands and your biceps. Relax the tension and feel the sensation of relief as it spreads throughout your arms.

12. Start by focusing on the neck and your facial muscles. Bring your chin gently towards your chest. Feel the strain on the neck's back Then, lift your head. Let your neck relax and

soften. Make your forehead wrinkle, close your eyes and tighten your jaw. You will feel tension on your face. Let these muscles relax, allowing your face to be smooth and relaxed.

13. Take a second to take a look at your body in general. Find any areas that are still causing tension, and then ease them. This will allow the feeling of deep relaxation that can permeate all of your body.

14. You can lie down or sit in a comfortable position and breathe in slowly and steadily for a couple of minutes, and allow you to let go and relax. Enjoy the peaceful sensation of your body.

15. Once you are ready, gradually relax your eyes, then relax then slowly return to your normal routine.

Guided Imagery for Healing and Restoring Calm

Guided imagery is an effective technique that has been proven to be effective when it comes to Cognitive Processing Therapy (CPT) to treat PTSD. It lets people engage their mind to construct the perfect, peaceful and calming mental space. This practice will lead you through an guided imagery exercise that will assist you in relaxing, finding your inner strength and encourage emotional recovery within the framework of your CPT process.

1. Find a peaceful and comfy area to lay or sit down. You must ensure that you aren't interrupted throughout the duration of this workout.

2. Relax your eyes, and breathe deeply taking a slow inhalation and exhaling all tension or anxieties every breath.

3. Imagine yourself in a peaceful and peaceful spot that you like. You could go to a sandy beach, a wooded area or meadow any place that provides you with peace and security.

4. Take note of the particulars in this serene area. Be aware of the colors, patterns, and the delicate motions of the surroundings.

5. Make yourself aware. What are you hearing at this location? Do you hear birds singing, waves breaking and leaves blowing on the wind? Let the sound provide a relaxing soundscape.

6. It is important to take a moment and notice the scents that are present in this area. Relax and think of the soothing scent that surrounds you within this serene space.

7. Experience the temperature as well as the feeling of the air against your skin. Do you feel warm and inviting or refreshing and cool? Feel the sensation and give you the feeling of relaxation.

8. While you are immersed into this meditation, you will be aware of a soft warmth that surrounds your body. This light will symbolize the healing power of love and heal, encompassing the entirety of your being.

9. Every breath you take, you will you will feel the healing light growing within you,

extending across every cell and fiber of your being. It will help you relax and healing any wounds or emotional hurt.

10. Imagine the presence of a compassionate and wise guide appearing within your visualisation. It could be any shape that is appealing to you, such as an animal, person or an abstract image. Use your senses to discern the guide.

11. Begin to talk with your guide and feel the unwavering support and wisdom they provide. Your guide can provide any advice or guidance that you require on the path to healing.

12. Pay attention to the response of your guide in the form of gesturing, words, or a simple presence. Remember that they're here to assist and support the way through this experience.

Chapter 9: Enhancing Emotional Regulation

The improvement of the ability to regulate emotions is an essential therapeutic component for people suffering from problems with their emotional regulation, which includes those suffering from the post-traumatic stress disorder (PTSD). This chapter outlines strategies for determine and address emotional triggers, skills for emotion regulation education, and enhancing awareness of emotions to help improve emotion regulation.

Identifying and Managing Triggers

The first step towards improving emotional regulation is to determine the triggers that contribute to the disorder of emotional regulation. Triggers may be either external (such like memories, thoughts) as well as external (such as particular situations or individuals). In identifying triggers people can be able to identify the particular circumstances that trigger emotional reactions.

When triggers are identified the individual can come up with strategies to deal with and manage efficiently. It could involve cognitive strategies like challenging negative thinking and engaging in self-talk that is positive. This could also include behavioral techniques like assertiveness training or seeking out social support. With these techniques they can decrease the effects of triggers that affect their emotional wellbeing and general well-being.

Emotion Regulation Skills Training

Training in emotional regulation is an essential component of improving emotional regulation. This includes learning and practicing specific techniques to control and regulate emotions efficiently. They can be classified in a variety of types:

1. The techniques for self-soothing can help people calm when they are experiencing

heightened feelings. For instance, deep breathing exercises or engaging in calming activities (e.g. or listening to soothing music, having a relaxing bath) as well as visualizing the peace and security of a place.

2. Strategies to manage stress: Distress tolerance strategies aid individuals in coping with difficult emotions, without resorting to destructive behaviours. They include exercises to ground yourself (e.g. paying attention to what is happening that are present) or using techniques to distract yourself (e.g. participating with a physical or a pastime exercise) as well as the power of self-compassion as well as acceptance.

3. Cognitive reappraisal Reframe and re-interpreting events to change the emotion produced. In challenging destructive or negative thoughts, people can change their perspectives and decrease the severity of their emotional responses.

Increasing Emotional Awareness

Enhancing consciousness of emotion is an important aspect of improving emotional regulation. People with issues with their emotional regulation struggle with accurately identifying and understanding their emotional state. Learning to develop emotional awareness means the ability to identify and categorize emotions in a precise manner, comprehending the physiological triggers and sensations that are associated with various emotions, as well as distinguishing between the primary and secondary emotions.

Meditation practices such as mindfulness as well as journaling are a great way to improve their emotional focus. Meditation that is mindful involves being present and in the moment, taking note of your own experiences, and emotions, and not judging. Journaling allows people to think about and examine their feelings and feelings, allowing them to increase the understanding of themselves and grow in self-awareness.

In boosting emotional awareness people can have better control of their emotions and take more educated decisions on how they can manage their emotions successfully.

Chapter 10: Building And Restoring Relationships

The ability to build and maintain relations is an integral part of healing for people suffering from Post-traumatic Stress Disorder (PTSD) as well as the people who love them. This chapter is focused on strategies to effectively communicate regarding PTSD building connections and trust, setting healthy boundaries and creating friendships that are supportive.

Communication with Loved Ones about PTSD

Honest and transparent communication is essential when talking about PTSD with your loved ones. Here are some guidelines to use effective communication

1. Offer education: Begin with sharing details about PTSD and its signs, symptoms as well as triggers as well as treatment options. Helping loved ones comprehend the challenges and experiences confronted by people suffering from PTSD.

2. Feelings and desires People suffering from PTSD should be encouraged to communicate openly their thoughts and concerns to family members and friends. This will help build compassion and understanding in the relationships.

3. Listening actively: Family members are expected to listen attentively without judgement or interruption. Making a secure space for people suffering from PTSD to be themselves allows for an open and honest dialogue, which strengthens the bond between them.

4. The ability to be patient and compassionate: Family members and loved family members should have patience and empathetic when talking about the issue of PTSD. This will help to provide a non-judgmental and positive atmosphere.

Rebuilding Trust and Connection

The effects of PTSD may cause tension in relationships and undermine trust among individuals. The process of rebuilding trust takes time. process. The methods listed below can help:

1. Recognizing triggers and reactions Family members should be educated on the triggers and responses related to the condition of PTSD. They can recognize and understand the person's reactions.

2. Communication that is consistent and open: Inspire people suffering from PTSD as well as their families to have ongoing discussions regarding their personal needs, limitations and issues. Communication regularly can build trust and build a stronger bond.

3. Be patient and supportive: Family members and loved family members should show patience and provide support throughout recovery. It could involve offering reassurance and support, taking part in therapy sessions or taking part in activities to promote peace and well-being.

4. Making positive memories Participating in positive events can build trust and make new memories. Concentrating on activities that create a feeling of belonging is essential.

Healthy Boundaries and Supportive Relationships

Setting healthy boundaries is crucial for those suffering from PTSD as well as their families. These are a few things to consider:

1. Respectful and transparent communication Create clear boundaries with transparent and respectful communications. It is also a good idea to discuss personal limitations requirements, personal expectations, as well as individual demands.

2. Self-care: Help people suffering from PTSD as well as their family members to focus on self-care in order to ensure the physical and mental health of their loved ones. Being self-careful allows individuals to set and sustain the healthy boundaries.

3. Find help from professionals in situations where the process of it becomes difficult to set boundaries and you need help from an expert like couples therapy can be beneficial. Therapists are able to provide advice and help in managing relationships.

4. Support networks: Help people suffering from PTSD and loved ones to get connected with support networks such as groups for support or online communities. They can offer support, guidance and also a feeling being part of.

Chapter 11: Addressing Sleep Disturbances

Sleep disturbances are a crucial aspect for treating post-traumatic stress disorder (PTSD). This chapter is focused on understanding the connection with PTSD as well as sleep. It also discusses setting up an appropriate sleep schedule, as well as managing insomnia and nightmares.

Understanding the Relationship Between Sleep and PTSD

Sleep disturbances and PTSD often are inextricably linked. The sleep disturbances may be as a result and a sign of suffering from PTSD. These factors can are a part of the connection between PTSD and sleep disturbances:

1. Hyperarousal Symptoms: The symptoms of hyperarousal associated with PTSD like an increased level of hypervigilance or vigilance could make it difficult to fall asleep and relax.

2. Nightmares: Nightmares can be a frequent manifestation of PTSD and may cause periodic awakenings throughout the night. This can lead to disturbances in sleep.

3. Intrusive thoughts and memories The thoughts and memories of intrusive people or those of the trauma are able to invade the minds of individuals as they attempt to fall asleep and disrupt their sleeping quality.

4. Hypervigilance: Those suffering from PTSD frequently have trouble feeling safe when they sleep, resulting in an increased level of alertness, as well as a disturbed sleep.

Establishing a Sleep Routine

Establishing a regular sleep schedule is vital for those suffering from PTSD. Here are some strategies to aid in establishing a healthy sleep routine

1. Follow a strict routine of sleep: Establish an established schedule for your bedtime and time of wake-up regardless of the time on the

weekends. This can help control the body's internal clock, and encourages greater sleep.

2. Set up a relaxing and comfortable sleep space ensure that the bedroom is quiet, comfortable and dark. Utilize earplugs or eye masks and the use of white noise machines when needed. The bedroom should be that is devoted to sleeping.

3. Beware of activities that can stimulate your mind before you go to sleep Relaxation: Take part in activities to help promote a peaceful state of mind. It could be reading an ebook, relaxing in an ice bath or engaging in relaxation exercises.

4. Reduce exposure to electronic devices. Do not use electronic devices, including tablets and smartphones prior to bedtime. The blue light produced from these devices could disrupt the process of producing hormones to induce sleep.

Dealing with nightmares and Insomnia

Sleep disturbances, insomnia and nightmares are both common insomnia-related issues for people suffering from PTSD. Strategies to assist in overcoming these problems:

1. Nightmares:

a. Imagery therapy: Get the help of a professional who is trained in the art of imagery training therapy (IRT). This method involves altering the scene and practicing a different more relaxing and less traumatic end to the nightmare in the period of wakefulness.

b. Relaxation methods: Try relaxing techniques prior to bedtime including deep breathing or gradual muscle relaxation. This can help lower anxiety and encourage a more peaceful sleeping.

C. Making a relaxing time to sleep: Develop an unwinding routine prior to bed that includes activities such as writing positive thoughts, reading or listening to relaxing music. It can to create a calm and peaceful environment before going to the bed.

2. Insomnia:

It is. Cognitive Behavioral Therapy for insomnia (CBT-I) It is recommended to seek treatment from a professional who is trained for CBT-I. The therapy is focused on the identification and modification of negative thoughts and behavior that contribute to sleepiness.

b. Habits to maintain a clean and healthy sleeping environment: Follow healthy sleep hygiene habits including avoiding coffee or eating large meals prior to bedtime, and limiting the time spent napping as well as creating a relaxing sleeping environment.

C. Consult a health professional: Discuss with an expert in healthcare for a discussion of possible medication or alternative therapies (e.g. herbal supplements) which may ease insomnia, if your other options do not work.

Chapter 12: Treating Comorbid Conditions

Treatment of co-occurring conditions is vital for effective management of post-traumatic stress disorder (PTSD) and improving overall wellbeing. This chapter examines methods for dealing with common comorbidities such as anxiety and depression, substance abuse, the trauma-related PTSD and Dissociative disorders.

Addressing Depression and Anxiety

Anxiety and depression often coexist together with PTSD and require an extensive approach to treatment. Here are some ways to treat these disorders:

1.   Psychotherapy: Cognitive-behavioral Therapy (CBT) successfully treats anxiety and depression. CBT can help individuals recognize and alter negative thoughts patterns, improve coping abilities as well as challenge negative beliefs.

2. Treatment: Antidepressant and anti-anxiety medication may be prescribed as part of therapy to ease symptoms. Consulting with a doctor is vital to figure out the best medication for you and dosage.

3. Changes in lifestyle: Inspire people to be active, learn methods of relaxation (e.g. meditation, deep breathing) and develop an appropriate sleep schedule. The lifestyle modifications will positively affect mood and anxiety levels.

4. Networks of support: Strong relationships help manage anxiety and depression. Inspire people to join support groups and seek assistance from family and friends.

Substance Abuse and PTSD

Abuse of substances and PTSD are often interspersed, and some people turn to drugs to cope with difficult events. The treatment of both disorders is vital in ensuring a full healing. Think about the following strategies:

1. Integrative treatment: Look for treatment programs that treat the co-occurring issues of PTSD as well as substance abuse. Integrative treatments offer a holistic method that treats both in a coordinated manner.

2. Therapy: Evidence-based treatments including cognitive-behavioral therapy (CBT) helps patients understand the underlying factors that lead to substance abuse, and devise healthy strategies for coping to deal with PTSD as well as addiction.

3. The use of medication-assisted therapy: In a few situations, medications-assisted therapy can be utilized to tackle problems with substance abuse. Drugs like naltrexone buprenorphine and methadone could benefit under the supervision by healthcare professionals.

4. Peer support groups: Inspire members to participate in peer support groups for example, Alcoholics Anonymous (AA) or Narcotics Anonymous (NA). These support groups offer a welcoming atmosphere for

people to talk about their stories, learn from each other, and also receive support.

Trauma and Dissociative Disorders

Disorders of dissociation and trauma often occur in conjunction with PTSD that require special treatments. Take note of the following methods:

1. Therapy that focuses on trauma, such as Eye Movement Desensitization and Processing (EMDR) or Trauma-focused Cognitive Behavioral Therapy (TF-CBT) are effective in addressing the effects of trauma as well as dissociative disorders. They help people process the trauma and build ways to cope.

2. Techniques for grounding: Help people who suffer from dissociative symptoms to learn methods of grounding to be in the actual moment. For instance, breathing exercises that are deep and focusing on the sensory experience and using objects that are tactile to anchor the body.

3. The work of inner-child therapy: addressing dissociative problems may require working with the inner child under the supervision of an therapist. The therapy approach can help individuals to heal their past hurts as well as increase self-confidence and self-love.

4. Certain instances medications may be prescribed to treat symptoms related to distress and dissociative disorder. A consultation with a medical professional is vital to establish the appropriateness of medication and its potential positive effects.

Chapter 13: Self-Care And Lifestyle Changes

Changes in lifestyle and self-care can be essential to promoting health and well-being of people with the post-traumatic stress disorder (PTSD). This chapter discusses ways to including healthy lifestyles and exercises and recognizing the significance of self-compassion as well as implementing self-care routines.

Promoting Overall Well-being

The promotion of overall wellness requires an approach that is holistic to overall health that includes physical, mental and emotional factors. Think about the following methods:

1. Physical exercise Physical activity: Regular exercise, for example, running, walking or even yoga can aid in reducing symptoms of PTSD and improve mood and boost overall fitness levels.

2. Healthy nutrition that is balanced: A nutritious, well-balanced diet that includes

vegetables, fruits, and healthy proteins and whole grain foods provides vital nutrients that are essential to maintaining the mental and physical health of your body. Eliminating processed foods as well as sugary snacks and caffeine may improve your overall health.

3. Sleeping well is crucial for people suffering from PTSD. Implementing a routine for sleep as well as creating a tranquil sleeping environment and incorporating relaxing before bed will increase the quality of sleep and overall wellbeing.

4. Management of stress: Implementing strategies for managing stress like meditation, deep breathing exercises, mindfulness meditation or participating in a variety of activities can help people manage stress and lessen the effects of PTSD symptoms.

Incorporating Healthy Habits and Activities

The incorporation of healthy practices and routines creates a sense of meaning satisfaction, joy, and fulfillment. Below are a few strategies to take into consideration:

1. Find hobbies and other interests They should encourage people suffering from PTSD to engage in hobbies such as playing an instrument such as painting, gardening or even writing. Participating in activities can give an uplifting feeling and a sense of calm.

2. Engage with nature: Taking in the outdoors and interacting with nature can have therapeutic effects. Being in the nature, horticulture or just sitting outside in the park can improve relaxation, ease anxiety, and boost the mood.

3. Learn techniques for relaxation and mindfulness Initiate people to meditation techniques and deep breathing exercises or gradual muscle relaxation. These methods help people develop feelings of tranquility as well as reduce stress and improve self-awareness.

4. Expression of creativity: Inspire people to discover creative ways of expression for expression, including the arts, writing or even music. Expression of creativity can be an outlet for healing and catharsis that allows people to express themselves and reflect on their experiences in a way that is unique.

Importance of Self-Compassion and Self-Care Practices

Self-compassion, self-care and compassion are crucial to navigating the difficulties of PTSD. Take note of the following techniques:

1. Develop self-compassion by encouraging people to practice self-compassion through speaking with kindness to oneself, acknowledging the efforts they have made, and practicing self-forgiveness. Make them aware that they are worthy of kindness and empathy.

2. Learn to set boundaries: Instruct individuals how important it is to establish limits to ensure their wellbeing. Instructing them on

how to recognize the limits of their abilities, share their desires, and saying"no" whenever necessary promotes self-care and respect for self.

3. Find social support: Inspire people to rely on your support networks that include trusted relatives, friends, or even support groups. Social connections provide validation as well as understanding and a sense of community.

4. Participate in self-care activities Assist individuals in developing routines and self-care rituals that focus on making sure they are focusing on their physical and emotional health. These could include activities such as relaxing baths and journaling, or practicing self-reflection or participating with mindful pursuits.

Chapter 14: Session Guide To Cognitive Processing Therapy Cpt

The Session-by -Session Handbook to CPT gives you a structured guideline to implement Cognitive Processing Therapy as part of your PTSD therapy journey. The goal of this guide is to provide the main goals, methods as well as activities that are required for every session. The sessions begin in Session 1: Introduction to CPT and Orienting toward traumatizing events, then Sessions 2: Recognizing and understanding thoughts and feelings before concluding by identifying and challenging trauma-related thoughts. A trained professional or therapist when participating in these sessions is vital for an optimal level of guidance, support and advancement.

Session 1: Introducing CPT and Orienting to Traumatic Events

Scope: The purpose for the initial session is to present Cognitive Processing Therapy, provide an overview of its goals and structure, as well as to guide the client through their traumatizing experiences.

1. Begin by introducing the client. Establish an environment that is safe and comfortable. Make sure to allow time for any required building of rapport.

2. Instruct the client on Cognitive Processing Therapy and its scientifically-based method of treating PTSD. The therapy is based on the connection between thought actions, emotions and thoughts for healing.

3. Consider the objectives of CPT that could include reduce the burden of symptoms related to trauma, improving the quality of life, and increasing the overall health.

4. Give an overview of scheduled sessions. Make clear the fact that CPT is a team-based process that involves the therapist and the patient. are working together to reach the same goals in treatment.

5. Find out how the client's perspective and appreciation for their trauma experiences.

Encourage them to talk about the experiences they have experienced while offering an environment that is supportive and not judging for them to be themselves.

6. Explain the concept of stuck points and explain why negative beliefs and thoughts can cause distress or avoidance and psychological issues. Help the patient to determine those initial points of contention that are related to the trauma they have experienced.

7. Start the writing process In this exercise, the participant is instructed to record the traumatic event(s) and in depth. Encourage them to concentrate on their thoughts, feelings and ideas that relate to the experience. The students should be writing for about 10 minutes each day and encourage further investigation of those stuck areas.

8. Offer the client psychoeducation about managing their distress in between sessions, introducing self-care techniques and grounding strategies to assist in coping with

emotional issues that be triggered during therapy.

9. End the session by reviewing the major points of discussion. Stress the importance of the client's participation and participation in the recovery process. Answer any concerns or questions clients may have concerning the treatment.

Session 2: Recognizing and Understanding Thoughts and Feelings

Goal: The goal for the second session is helping clients understand the connections between their thoughts, feelings and actions while gaining insight on how these influences affect the other.

1. Examine the story the student has composed during the session before. Examine their experiences of participating with the writing task along with the difficulties they encountered as well as new knowledge acquired.

2. Present the Cognitive Model and explain how the things trigger thought patterns, and trigger emotions and behavior. Let the client know how these aspects interact and their experience of trauma.

3. Engage in a discussion about the patterns of negative thinking in your client and how they can cause distress and affect everyday functioning. Share examples of the most common mental distortions (e.g. thoughts of all-or-nothing or excessive generalization) and help your client to spot these in their thinking patterns.

4. Make use of to use the Thought Record worksheet to Teach clients to spot and combat negative thinking. Help them identify certain scenarios, emotions, and thoughts and behaviors that follow, showing them how to analyze the evidence to support and refute the thoughts.

5. Instruct the client to engage in mental challenges in therapy sessions as well as within their everyday life. Make sure to

emphasize the need for regular training to improve this ability.

6. Resolve any emotional responses or issues that might be triggered by challenging or challenging thoughts. Recognize and help the emotional experiences of the client and provide guidance on strategies for self-regulation and managing stress.

7. Recap the most important points covered in the discussion and urge your client to keep writing stories and rethinking their ideas throughout the sessions. Offer resources or tasks for further research if required.

Session 3: Identifying and Challenging Trauma-Related Thoughts

Scope: The purpose of the 3rd session is to explore and rethinking clients' thoughts about trauma and their impact on them and feelings, focusing on the stuck areas found in the accounts.

1. Start by reviewing the clients' story and journey to identify stuck points from the

previous session. Look for patterns that are emerging or patterns in their thinking and their beliefs.

2. Examine The Thought Record process and ensure the client's confidence in implementing the procedure. Instruct the client to provide the issues they've identified and dealt on during sessions.

3. Choose with your team some or two important stuck areas to further investigate. Help the client to explore the evidence in support and against these ideas, helping clients gain a better viewpoint.

4. Present to the ABC Worksheet (Activating the event and Consequences of Beliefs) for further exploration of the connection between certain things, beliefs, and emotional responses. Help the child finish the chosen blocked point(s) sheet.

5. Help the client to generate different, more balanced ideas about the underlying point(s). Give support and advice through the entire

process and challenge any mental issues that occur.

6. Instruct the client to engage in alternative thinking and to challenge their thinking in actual scenarios. Talk about any achievements or difficulties they've encountered in the process.

7. Resolve any emotional responses or issues during the difficult procedure, using grounding or self-care methods to help the individual.

8. Review the main points of the session and acknowledge the progress of your client. It is important to encourage them to keep independent work using ABC Worksheet and the Thought Record and ABC Worksheet for any additional issues.

Session 4: Cognitive Restructuring: Changing Unhelpful Beliefs

Scope: The purpose of the 4th session is to concentrate on cognitive restructuring. It is aimed to take on and change negative beliefs that are related to the trauma event(s) and the related thinking.

1. Start the session by reviewing how the client has progressed in the past session. Examine their thoughts on problems and discuss any insight or shifts they've noticed with regards to their thinking and belief habits.

2. Highlight the significance of cognitive restructuring to alter harmful beliefs and encouraging long-term healing. Discuss how cognitive restructuring can help change belief patterns that contribute to stress and negative feelings.

3. Explain the concept of basic beliefs that are deeply embedded views about self as well as the world. The client should be able to understand what traumatic events may influence their beliefs.

4. Use the diagram of the Cognitive Triangle to demonstrate the interrelationships between emotions, thoughts and behavior.

Examine how changing thoughts can positively affect emotions and behavior.

5. Select one particular belief that is harmful associated with the trauma that you will be focused on during the session. Help the client to examine the evidence in support of and against this conviction, and encourage them to question their irrational or flawed thinking.

6. Aid the client in developing new and balanced thoughts that are consistent with their present situation and objectives. Encourage them to develop authentic and self-affirming assertions.

7. Make use of positive self-talk and affirmations in therapy sessions, and for homework in between sessions. Help them integrate these new ideas in their everyday lives for a stronger reinforcement of the change.

8. Discuss any reactions to emotions or problems that could occur when challenging or changing the beliefs. Help the client to

understand and accept their emotional state, providing methods for self-care and emotional regulation.

9. Review the most important points covered during the meeting and discuss the progress made by your client through their process of brain transformation. It is important to encourage them to keep making changes to their unhelpful beliefs, and replacing those with more adaptable ones.

Session 5: Introduction to Exposure Techniques

Fifth session will introduce methods of exposure, that involve confronting fears, and slowly reducing the fear of traumatic experiences as well as situations that are associated with the trauma.

1. Start with a discussion of the goal and the principles behind exposure therapy. It is important to explain that exposure can lessen fear and reduce avoidance by moderate and

gradual exposure to stimuli that are related to trauma.

2. Make sure that the the exposure will take place in a comfortable manner and ensure their security and safety throughout the procedure.

3. Engage in a discussion about the behavior of your client as well as their effect on everyday performance. Make sure they understand the relationship between avoidance and maintenance in PTSD symptoms.

4. Inform the patient about diverse methods for exposure that are available, including both in vivo and imaginal exposure. Instruct the client that imaginal exposure involves reviewing and discussing trauma-related memories as opposed to in-vivo exposure, which is the process of addressing avoided scenarios or triggers associated with the trauma.

5. Create an exposure hierarchy with the help of a team. Together with the client, find a wide range of situations or stimuli that are trauma-related which trigger the least amount of anxiety to the most difficult.

6. Examine the reasons for exposure therapy and discuss the way that repeatedly exposed exposure aids in retraining your brain's responses to traumatic memories as well as triggers.

7. Learn relaxation techniques for the client like deep breathing and progressive muscle relaxation. These can be utilized for coping strategies during the exercises of exposure.

8. Introduce the idea self-monitoring. Encourage the patient to keep track of their stress levels as well as sub-conscious unit of distress (SUDs) as they engage with activities that expose them to stress.

9. Assignment of exposure assignments to the client beginning by introducing the most anxiety-inducing item in the list of items.

Explain how they can move forward and slowly expose the client to the trigger or the situation.

10. Answer any questions or concerns clients may have regarding the process of exposure and supply the client with tools or resources to help them handle any anxiety that may be triggered.

Session 6: Gradual Exposure: Imaginal and In Vivo Exercises

Ziel: The purpose of the 6th session is to teach the gradual exposure technique and to practice it that specifically employ the imaginal as well as in-vivo techniques that help clients to process and confront trauma-related memories.

1. The session begins by re-reading your client's experience with the exercises for exposure that were assigned during the session prior to it. Discuss any issues that they experienced, shifts in their anxiety levels and overall thoughts.

2. Explain the idea of imaginal exposure. This is where the patient recollects and vividly recollects the trauma experience in a secure and secure environment. Discuss how this method can reduce the intensity of emotions that is associated with incident.

3. Consider the importance to create a safe and tranquil environment prior to participating in an imaginal exercise. Introduce relaxation strategies which can help reduce anxiety while exercising.

4. The client is guided through an imaginal exposure practice. The client is asked to recount the trauma in every detail that they can starting from the point of no return. Help them engage their emotions and senses during the process of recounting.

5. Explore any feelings, thoughts or physical sensations which are triggered during the practice. Facilitate the process of letting go and redefine their experiences by challenging any negative notions that might surface.

6. Introduce the concept of in-vivo exposure where you are gradually exposed to the real world situations and triggers with the traumatic incident. Consider the necessity of beginning with less depressing scenarios then moving into more demanding scenarios.

7. With the client, make an in-vivo strategy for exposure that follows the fear hierarchy created in the earlier sessions. Assist them in identifying specific scenarios or triggers that they should be prepared to confront slowly.

8. Assignment of in-vivo exposure assignments to the student, with a focus on an environment that is less stressful in their hierarchy of fear. Help them to slowly confront the situation with relaxation methods and strategies for coping as required.

Session 7: Advanced Cognitive Restructuring Techniques

Goal: The seventh session is designed to teach advanced methods of cognitive restructuring to test the negative beliefs that are triggered by the trauma.

1. Start the session by reviewing the progress of your client and their experiences through exposure exercises. Inquire about changes in their beliefs or patterns of thought from the last session.

2. Examine the fundamental strategies for cognitive restructuring that were taught in previous sessions like analyzing data of cognitive distortions and developing reasonable opinions.

3. Include additional sophisticated strategies for cognitive restructuring including cost-benefit analyses, de-strophizing and looking at the validity of beliefs that are negative. Discuss how these methods aid in challenging the unhelpful beliefs.

4. Help the client apply these techniques that are advanced to perceived negative thoughts. Help them develop judgmental thinking to consider the advantages and risks of

sustaining these beliefs. ask questions about catastrophic thinking and assess the validity of their beliefs.

5. Aid the client to identify and dispel any fundamental notions or beliefs that contribute to the unhelpful patterns of thinking. Aid them in changing their assumptions to make them more flexible and healthy for their wellbeing.

6. Stress the importance of practicing sophisticated cognitive techniques on a regular basis. Instruct the client to integrate the techniques in their daily lives and to use them every time they are confronted with negative or destructive thinking patterns.

7. Give supportive feedback and encouragement of the progress made by the client in challenging their perceptions. Recognize their effort and perseverance through this entire process.

Session 8: Enhancing Emotional Processing and Closure, Termination, and Relapse Prevention Strategies

Ziel: The aim of the 8th session is to enhance the emotional process, reaching closure as well as preparing for the end of therapy, while discussing methods to avoid Relapse.

1. Start the session with a reflection on the clients' progress through therapy as well as the experiences they have had with the process of exposure, cognitive restructuring and various other strategies. Recognize their achievements and perseverance.

2. Investigate the emotional response of the trauma as well as the emotions that came up through therapy. Inspire clients to share and acknowledge their feelings and help them heal.

3. Explore the idea of reaching closure as well as the readiness of the client to begin this process of therapy. It is important to clarify that closing does not necessarily mean

forgetting about the experience, but rather achieving acceptance and the integration.

4. Work with the client in order to determine any unresolved problems or issues that need to be resolved prior to the end of therapy. Provide support, direction and other resources that can help the client navigate these difficulties.

5. Talk about strategies for preventing relapses, and create a strategy for the patient to make sure they are equipped with the support and tools they need for their improvement over the long run. This could involve identifying the potential causes, developing coping strategies as well as establishing the self-care regimen.

6. Re-examine the progress achieved through therapy, and make sure that clients are at ease with the conclusion of the therapy. Review their progress and resilience, enhancing the ability of them to continue their journey of healing on their own.

7. Include any additional information or suggestions that might help with ongoing support. Make it a priority to maintain your own self-care routine and seeking out expert assistance should you need it later on.

8. In conclusion, express gratitude to the client for their therapy involvement and recognizing the strength and dedication towards recovery.

Chapter 15: Thriving And Post-Traumatic Growth

When confronted with Post-traumatic Stress Disorder (PTSD) It is possible to overcome and even thrive. The chapter focuses on the idea of post-traumatic development, discovering an identity and meaning, developing resilience and establishing the foundation for a new existence in the aftermath of an experience of trauma.

Finding Meaning and Purpose

The search for meaning and a purpose following the trauma may lead to satisfaction and wellbeing. Think about the following strategies:

1. Review the incident Inviting people to look back on the trauma they experienced and examine how it affected their beliefs, values and goals. Introspection can help individuals gain new insight and understanding throughout their life.

2. Get support: Participate in discussions with your trusted friends family members, therapists, or friends to help you process and understand the impact of the experience. The sharing of experiences and views may provide new perspectives and aid in the process of determining meaning.

3. Participate in activities that are altruistic by performing acts of kindness or giving back to others will give you an inner sense of satisfaction and satisfaction. It is a good idea to encourage people to engage in voluntary work, assist organizations, or participate in community projects.

4. Create goals that are aligned with your values: Help individuals with creating goals that have meaning and aligned with their beliefs. It can give one with a sense of direction as well as the motivation to take action.

Cultivating Resilience

Resilience is crucial for overcoming the obstacles of PTSD and undergoing expansion. Take note of the following methods:

1. Create a positive attitude Inspire people to adopt positive thinking, confront any negative thinking, and to reframe the way they think. Instilling confidence and optimism can help one cope against challenges.

2. Create a network of support Develop relationships and establish connections with people who are supportive and offer emotional support and encouragement through difficult times. Create a sense of belonging and sense of belonging.

3. Self-care is a priority: Make it a point to prioritize self-care exercises and healthy eating. Also, get enough rest, and relaxation methods. Being aware of your mental and physical health can boost resilience and the ability to cope.

4. Accept adaptability: Encourage individuals to improve their flexibility of thought and

behaviour. Help them adapt to changing situations, gain from the challenges they face, and come up with inventive solutions.

Building a New Life After Trauma

Rebuilding your life following the trauma requires growth, perseverance and a satisfying future. Take a look at the following suggestions:

1. Set up a support network Make sure that you surround yourself with a solid community of friends who are trustworthy and family members, as well as groups of support. These relationships can be a source of assistance and support throughout the process of recovery.

2. Find professional advice: Recommend people to participate in sessions of counseling or therapy in order to resolve any unresolved traumas. They can also develop the ability to cope, and create strategies for moving ahead.

3. Create realistic goals: Help people in setting goals that are in line with their goals and

ideals. By breaking down goals into manageable actions can give a feeling of achievement and progress.

4. Explore new possibilities: Inspire individuals to discover new hobbies, interests in hobbies, careers, or other pursuits which align with their interests and ideals. The pursuit of new opportunities can lead to personal growth as well as a new feeling of meaning.

Chapter 16: Case Studies And Exemplars

Case studies can provide useful insights regarding the use of Cognitive Processing Therapy (CPT) as well as its efficacy in the treatment of Post-Traumatic Stress Disorder (PTSD). This chapter will will present three case studies which illustrate the steps involved in assessing treatments, as well as overcome the obstacles within CPT. Case Study 1 demonstrates the success of the treatment from diagnosis to completion of therapy. Case Study 2 highlights the issues and difficulties encountered during therapy and strategies used to conquer roadblocks. Case Study 3 showcases the integrated approach used by CPT to address the complex nature of PTSD. The case studies are examples of the effectiveness of CPT and its ability to be adapted to each individual's requirements.

Case Study 1: From Assessment to Successful Treatment:

The case study focuses on Case Study 1, a female victim of a vehicle accident experiences signs of PTSD with a host of symptoms, such as intrusive thoughts of the accident, avoiding, and heightened anxiety. The therapist conducts a thorough examination, collecting information on the event that caused the trauma as well as the client's symptomatology as well as her therapy goals. Following the evaluation, CPT is identified as the most appropriate therapy approach. The doctor introduces CPT and provides psychoeducation regarding the effects of trauma on emotions and cognition. Through structured sessions of CPT clients learn to challenge and identify the negative thoughts that she has about the accident. The client gradually replaces her distorted beliefs with more realistic and adaptive thoughts, which reduces anxiety as well as enhancing the overall quality of her life. This case illustrates the efficacy of CPT to guide a patient through assessment and results in treatment.

Case Study 2: Overcoming Treatment Challenges and Roadblocks:

Case Study 2 presents a male veteran of the military with his own history of suffering from trauma in combat. In the first few sessions of CPT the patient experiences problems with the cognitive process because of emotional stress and avoidance. The clinician is aware of the necessity for flexibility and uses an approach of gradual opening up and cognitive restructuring. The patient is invited to share his fears and anxieties about engaging the emotions and thoughts associated with trauma. The therapist introduces the techniques of relaxation and grounding for improving emotional regulation. The patient is more likely to process and confront traumatizing memories through building confidence and creating a secure therapy setting. The story highlights the importance in adjusting strategies to deal with the obstacles and challenges to treatment in order to increase client involvement and improvement.

Case Study 3: CPT as an Integrative Approach in Complex PTSD:

in Case Study 3, a woman who has survived childhood abuse suffers from Complex PTSD. It is characterized by an intricate interplay between chronic trauma-related symptoms as well as comorbid ailments. The doctor employs an integrative method, which combines CPT alongside other interventions based on evidence. CPT can be used to treat the most fundamental signs of PTSD and also incorporates additional strategies for addressing dissociation, emotions dysfunction, and issues in interactions. The practitioner works closely with the client in establishing an extensive treatment program that incorporates different therapeutic approaches. The scenario demonstrates the flexibility and flexibility of CPT in its integrative method to address the complex nature of Complex PTSD, providing a complete treatment strategy to the patient.

Case studies can provide useful insights on the effectiveness and application that can be derived from Cognitive Processing Therapy (CPT) to treat Post-Traumatic Stress Disorder

(PTSD). In Case Study 1, we examine the progress from diagnosis to positive treatment results and highlight the pattern-based structure of CPT. The Case Study 2 illustrates the importance in adjusting treatment strategies to address obstacles and challenges in order to encourage client involvement and growth. The case Study 3 demonstrates the integrative method that is the basis of CPT to address the complexity of the disorder known as Complex PTSD and demonstrates the flexibility in CPT as a holistic treatment option. These case studies illustrate the effectiveness of CPT and its capability to cater for specific needs of individuals, leading clients to healing, perseverance, and a better quality of life.

Chapter 17: Understanding Complex Ptsd

Hey, I'm Peace J Williams, and this week we'll be exploring the issue of "Understanding Complex PTSD." A disorder of anxiety that results due to prolonged exposure and stress, Complex PTSD differs from the more wellknown cousin, PTSD. Take a look at the signs, triggers as well as the main differences between them, and shed the light on this frequently misunderstood disorder. By examining this topic will help us improve understanding and increase empathy for people suffering from Complex PTSD. We can begin this journey with you.

1.1 Defining Complex PTSD

Complex posttraumatic stress disorder (complex PTSD), often called cPTSD also known as CPTSD it is a psychological health issue which is characterised by a mixture of PTSD symptoms and other distressing signs. Additional symptoms could be difficulties in the regulation of emotions, increased levels of anger, as well as the feeling of a general insecurity towards the world.

To understand Complex PTSD better, it is crucial to come up with an accurate definition of this complex disorder. Complex PTSD, commonly referred to as CPTSD manifests as the result of persistent trauma for a long time, that causes a lot of emotional and psychological anxiety. Contrary to PTSD that typically results out of a single incident CPTSD results from continuous victimization, neglect, or repeated exposure to frightening incidents.

In this chapter we'll explore the key elements that comprise CPTSD. We will also explore the psychological and emotional impact it has on the sufferer. When we understand the distinct features of CPTSD and characteristics, we can make way to a deeper knowledge of the complexity of CPTSD and provide compassionate support for those suffering from the consequences. Begin by joining me in unravelling the intricate nature of this disorder and expand our knowledge of the issues facing those suffering from Complex PTSD.

1.2 Causes and Triggers

Complex PostTraumatic Stress Disorder (CPTSD) is believed to result from longterm and extreme abuse, that occurs repeatedly over a prolonged period. Most often, abuse takes place during the vulnerable years of the life of an individual, like early childhood or the adolescent years, causing difficulties throughout the course of their lives.

Stress from trauma profoundly affects the brain. Research concluding that it leads to permanent changes in brain areas, such as the hippocampus, amygdala and the prefrontal cortex. The alterations could have major effects on the individual's mental and emotional functioning.

CPTSD is triggered by a myriad of chronic or traumatic experiences, such as however not only:

1. Children are abused, neglected or even abandonment

2. Domestic violence

3. Genocide

4. Childhood soldiering

5. Torture

6. Slavery

In these tragic events The victim will often be in the hands of someone else and has no ability to flee easily which can increase the negative impact of abuse on their psychological wellbeing.

1.3 Symptoms and Diagnostic Criteria

In this article we will examine in detail the main characteristics that are characteristic of Complex PTSD and the specific diagnostic criteria. The understanding of the symptoms is vital in understanding the effect of trauma that is prolonged on an individual's psychological and mental wellbeing. Through examining the diagnosis criteria, we can gain knowledge of how doctors recognize and distinguish Complex PTSD from related ailments. Let's get down to unravel the complexity of these symptoms as well as diagnostic procedures, increasing our understanding of this crucial part of recovering.

Symptoms of CPTSD

CPTSD Symptoms extend over the basic symptoms of PTSD that involve experiencing relapses the symptoms of avoidance, hyperarousal, or avoidance. It encompasses a variety of traumatic experiences confirmed by studies (Cloitre and others. (2013)):

1. Emotional Dysregulation: People suffering from CPTSD typically have trouble controlling their moods, resulting in extreme anger, chronic depression, sadness or even thoughts of suicide.

2. A negative selfperception of CPTSD may cause a negative selfimage making people feel

helpless embarrassed, ashamed, or guilty. It is also possible that they perceive them as being fundamentally different to other people.

3. Problems with relationships: Issues with trust and selfperceptions that are negative can affect relationships. This can cause people to stay clear of them or in unhealthy patterns that they learned from previous situations.

4. Dissociation from Trauma: Certain sufferers may experience a disconnect between their own self (depersonalization) as well as the environment around them (derealization). In extreme instances it is possible that they experience an amnesia that is either complete or in part due to traumarelated events.

5. The loss of meaning caused by CPTSD may thwart one's basic convictions, values, religion, belief, and faith in the world as well as in other people.

They have an enormous influence on people's lives they live in, and can cause major impairments across a variety of areas, including social, familial, personal as well as educational aspects.

Diagnosis of CPTSD

In spite of its longstanding definition CPTSD isn't listed in the 5th edition of "Diagnostic and Statistical Manual of Mental Disorders" (DSM5) which is why it does not have official recognition by the American Psychiatric Association (APA).

Although CPTSD has distinctive symptoms, there is a consensus that the similarity to PTSD as well as other conditions related to trauma don't justify the need for a separate diagnosis. Therefore, the DSM5 classifies CPTSD' symptoms with the symptoms of PTSD.

But, a lot of mental health specialists do accept CPTSD as a separate diagnosis, because the typical signs of PTSD don't fully capture specific traits that are observed in people that have experienced repeated trauma.

Note This is because the World Health Organization (WHO) made a major step in 2018 by acknowledging CPTSD (Complex PostTraumatic Stress Disorder) as a distinct diagnosis within the 11th edition "International Statistical Classification of Diseases and Related Health Problems" (ICD11).

Since its fairly recently recognized and its absence from the DSM5 physicians may be able to be able to diagnose people with PTSD rather than complicated PTSD. Since there's no particular test that can distinguish between both, it's essential to be aware of your symptoms and relay the symptoms to your physician in order to ensure a thorough assessment.

The treatment methods for both disorders are the same, however it's important to address the additional signs and symptoms associated with the trauma you've suffered that your doctor or therapist must address.

Additionally, CPTSD can display signs and symptoms which are similar to Borderline personality disorder (BPD). Even though BPD does not always stem from the trauma of childhood, it's frequently linked to it. Certain psychologists and researchers propose adding BPD in the definition of CPTSD within future DSM editions in order to recognize this connection to trauma, encourage an improved knowledge of BPD and lessen the stigma associated with those who suffer from BPD.

Chapter 18: The Impact Of Trauma On The Mind And Body

We're back on our way to this New Complex PTSD Recovery Workbook. This chapter is called "The Impact of Trauma on the Mind and Body," we will explore the profound impacts that trauma can cause on our mental as well as physical wellbeing. By conducting a thorough examination of the subject, we will be able to comprehend the interconnectedness of our personal experiences as well as their impact on. Begin by exploring the way trauma impacts our bodies and minds opening the way to an holistic approach to rehabilitation and healing. We can begin this journey of discovery in a group.

2.1 Psychological Effects of Trauma

The psychological effects of trauma affect the psychological and mental wellbeing. Trauma can refer to a terrifying feeling that may be brought on by a myriad of circumstances, like violence, abuse or accidents, natural catastrophes or even witnessing an emotional incident. Trauma's psychological impact will differ from person to individual, however some typical response options are:

1. PostTraumatic Stress Disorder (PTSD) A single of the most widelypublicized emotional impacts that trauma sufferers experience is PTSD. The condition is characterized by the repeated reexperience memories of the traumatizing event via dreams, flashbacks, or thoughts that are intrusive. The sufferers of PTSD might also feel an emotional numbness, the absence of any reminders of the event, as well as increased arousal such as being easily scared or experiencing difficulty falling asleep.

2. Anxiety and panic disorders Trauma may cause greater anxiety as well as an increase in the chance of suffering from panic attacks. Patients may be overwhelmed with anxiety, fear and an unending sense of threat.

3. Depression: Traumas can cause emotions of despair, sadness as well as a decrease in enthusiasm for activities that once were

loved. Depression could be the consequence of the event itself or as a result of difficulty in dealing with the aftermath.

4. Dissociation: A few people may feel dissociation. This can be a feeling of disconnection from emotions, thoughts or their the environment as a means to deal with trauma. The result can be feeling detached or feeling like the events of one's life are not real.

5. Hyperarousal and Hypervigilance: Those who've been through traumas may be hypervigilant and constantly scanning their surroundings for dangers. Hyperarousal may cause difficulties in concentrating, as well as problems with sleeping.

6. The shame and guilt of survivors of trauma might feel shame or guilt, particularly when they feel that they are responsible for the trauma they experienced or feel ashamed by their reactions to emotions.

7. Substance Abuse A few people take to alcohol or drugs to deal with the emotional consequences of trauma. This can lead to substance abuse problems that could be a problem.

8. SelfHarm and suicidal thoughts People who have suffered trauma can take selfharming actions in an attempt to cope with their emotional trauma. Some people may also have suicidal thoughts because of despairing feelings that overwhelm them.

It is crucial to realize that not every person who suffers trauma will experience serious psychological issues or suffer from severe psychological effects. People can show resilience and cope strategies which allow them to heal from the trauma in the course of. But for people who experience severe mental distress, seeking assistance from a professional, like therapy or counseling can assist in understanding and coping with the emotional trauma. Support and early intervention from families and friends could help in the process of assisting recovery.

2.2 Physical Manifestations of Trauma

Traumarelated physical symptoms can vary and be multifaceted that reflect the complicated interaction between the brain, nervous system, as well as physical responses to trauma. Trauma can be classified as chronic or acute, and each one of them can trigger specific physiological reactions.

Traumas that are sudden and triggered by an unforeseen and serious situation, may trigger the infamous "fight or flight" response controlled by the sympathetic nervous system. When this happens, people are likely to experience increased heart rates and breathing speed, increased alertness and increased tension of muscles, all which help the body be alert to any threat. Stress hormones are released specifically cortisol and adrenaline can also contribute to the physiological changes.

However, ongoing trauma, caused by stress over a long period or continual adversity can result in a dysregulation of your autonomic nervous. The symptoms could be of increased arousal. This can manifest as persistent anxiety, insomnia, and difficulties in concentration. In addition, people may suffer physical symptoms like stomach issues, headaches, as well as a weak immune system as a result of prolonged contact with stress hormones.

Another common manifestation of trauma is the disruption of the hypothalamicpituitaryadrenal (HPA) axis, which controls the body's stress response. Trauma can cause disruption to this axis, leading to elevated cortisol levels as well as an diminished capacity to deal with stressful situations, possibly leading to various physical health issues.

Furthermore, the effects of trauma on the structure of the brain and its function has been well documented. Traumarelated experiences over and over can change areas of the brain which are responsible for emotional regulation processing of memories, as well as making decisions. This can lead to depression, anxiety and difficulties in building positive relationships.

It is crucial to understand that different people react to trauma differently and therefore, not all sufferers will display the same physical symptoms. Furthermore, symptoms could persist long after the trauma experience has been over or may require therapeutic intervention to help heal and healing.

In conclusion knowing the physical manifestations that trauma can cause is vital to provide adequate support and intervention for people who have suffered traumatizing incidents. When we recognize the interconnectedness between the body and the mind and the body, we will be able to increase our understanding of the impact trauma has on us and help develop better strategies for healing and resiliency.

2.3 The MindBody Connection

The complex connection between body and the mind is apparent when you are confronted with trauma. It can be difficult to determine the source of certain symptoms that can be manifest physically and emotionally. In the case of trauma, it could cause issues with focus, memory, or insomnia, making the person unsure of whether these symptoms stem due to physical or emotions.

Furthermore, traumatic stress may affect your diet and lead to unhealthy eating choices which could influence your sleep patterns and wellbeing. A stressinduced headache can be a part of this complicated interplay as the headacherelated pain could add to the stress level.

Chapter 19: Building A Foundation For Recovery

Like a sturdy base is vital to every construction, building a solid base is essential for healing of Complex PTSD. In these pages, we'll examine the essential components of selfcompassion and the cultivation of resilience, as well as establishing an emotional support system. When we explore these fundamental principles, we'll establish the groundwork for a comprehensive and transformative process of recovery. Let's get started and build the foundations to a better path in the future.

3.1: Embracing SelfCompassion and Radical Acceptance

For those who are dealing with complicated PTSD healing, a deep transformational shift starts by practicing selfcompassion as well as radical acceptance. When we begin this path to healing, it's essential to treat our own self with the same respect as we show patience, understanding, and compassion which we'd extend to an amiable friend who is struggling with their own challenges.

For a brief moment, imagine and cradling your heart with the soft hug of selflove. Selfcompassion is admitting our hurt and suffering with no judgment and giving us the soothing balm of compassion. This is a call to be present for our feelings and even those that are uncomfortable by embracing them with a heart that is open.

Accepting ourselves as selflove means acknowledging the vulnerability and scars that are an integral part of the human condition. This is an acknowledgement that the pain we experience is not a defining factor however it is an evidence of our resilience and resilience. Through cultivating a caring and nourishing connection with ourselves, we can create an area of security in which healing can take place.

Also crucial on this journey is practicing radical acceptance. The practice of radical acceptance requires us to be with ourselves as we are, and with no resistance or denial. It recognizes that our past is not changeable even if we be afflicted by the traumas of our past but we have the power to define the future of our lives.

Acceptance without a doubt isn't about accepting or acknowledging the pain we endure; instead it allows individuals to let go of the pressure of selfpity and the fight to redress what's already happened. It's a brave act of letting go to the reality of our experience while, at the same time getting free from the chains that hold us in the inner turmoil.

By incorporating mindfulness techniques, soft selfinquiry, as well as heartfelt intent and intention, we can learn to build a nurturing space inside our hearts, a sanctuary in which growth, healing and change can flourish.

Keep in mind, dear reader, that selfcompassion and total acceptance aren't destinations instead, they serve as lifelong companions in our path to difficult PTSD healing. If we can cultivate these characteristics inside ourselves, they open the way for an incredibly change that will take us to a point that is wounded to a state that is incredibly strong, resilient as well as a profound love for ourselves.

3.2 Cultivating Resilience

When we look for ways to heal through Complex PTSD, we encounter the notion of resilience as the power of resilience that lies in each one of us just waiting to be nurtured, and used to its fullest extent. As a robust plant is able to find its way through gaps in concrete, so do we have a pathway for healing through the obstacles which life throws at us.

Resilience isn't a static quality, but a dynamic procedure. It's the practice of stretching without breaking, of gaining the ability to move with the wind of change. Imagine a tree that is tall during a storm. Its branches might wiggle, but the roots of its trunk are strong giving unwavering assistance.

In our process of regaining control over our emotions We must take care of our own inner strength. We can explore a few strategies that are guided by an integrated approach which can assist us in cultivating and maintain this vital quality.

Nature's Wisdom: Embracing the Flow

Resilience, as its foundation requires adapting to the changing environment and recovering from the adversity. Nature can be our best guide for this purpose. As a river tries to find it's way through the obstacles in front of it, we too could master the changes and twists that life throws at us. By practicing mindfulness, including meditation and breathing allows us to tune in to our present and be in the flow of life's the flow.

Harnessing Inner Strength: SelfCompassion and Empowerment

To build resilience, it is essential to first build relationships with our own self. Consider speaking to yourself like you would speak to a close person with compassion as well as understanding and encouraging. Selfcompassion is the foundation of resilience. It provides an oasis of safety during tough moments. When we gain a sense of our own selfconfidence, we gain control over our story and build confidence that we are able to face our life's storms.

Community and Connection: Weaving a Web of Support

As the web of a spider is weaved in order to construct a solid framework, we can also create a support web. Establishing and maintaining connections to loved ones, family members or support groups may give us the feeling of belonging as well as security when problems occur. Being open about our experience and hearing the tales of others may provide us with a sense of belonging and remind us that we're never the only ones on this path.

The Dance of Resilience: Flexibility and Adaptability

Resilience is a combination of flexibleness and adaptability. Much like a professional dancer who is able to effortlessly adapt to the rhythm of music, we are able to adjust our reactions to the changing rhythms of life. Through meditation and meditation, we are able to take a moment, be aware and then choose the appropriate responses mindfully. This helps us shift from reacting to situations and to respond with intent.

Dear readers, fostering resilience is a process that takes practice, patience and selfcompassion. As a garden flourishes by nurturing as we develop and flourish by putting in the effort. While we continue along this road, keep in mind that you're not in the dark and your inherent resilience will be the guiding light, pointing you towards a space where you can heal and be whole.

3.3: Developing a Support Network

Within the complex tapestry of recovery of Complex PTSD, the importance of having a supportive network can't be understated. Like a tree receives nutrients from the earth, and from the warmth of sunshine, we as well, flourish in the presence of the loving presence of other people. Establishing and maintaining a support network is similar to taking care of the gardens of our souls. It is a process that requires a lot of effort, patience as well as the desire to extend a hand and be received.

The Power of Connection

Humans are social beings, wired to connect. But, the repercussions of emotional trauma is often a cause for feelings of loneliness and a feeling of disconnection from the world that surrounds us. The creation of a network of support is an effective remedy to feeling isolateda relief for the heart that is wounded. It offers a safe space in which the stories of our lives can be shared as well as our suffering acknowledged and our strengths praised.

Cultivating Your Tribe

Consider your support group as a wide range of friends who have their own special talents in your journey of healing. It could include family members, friends relatives, therapists, help groups and loved pets. As a garden flourishes thanks to a myriad of plant species and flowers, healing is enhanced when you're surrounded by those who help you grow.

Nurturing Reciprocity

The path to healing is not a singleway avenue. As you give and receive, you have also the ability to give. Sharing your knowledge, experiences and compassion with those who are part of your community could create an amazing mutuality that benefits both the giver and recipients. It is a way to remind yourself that you're not limited just by the scars you've experienced, you're an incredibly complex and resilient person who is with the capacity to love and give.

Honoring Boundaries and Consent

While you weave the threads that make up your community of friends you must respect your boundaries as well as the boundaries of those around you. Good relationships are built upon an underlying foundation of trust with respect, understanding, and compassion. Make sure you communicate your requirements in a clear and transparent manner and invite those within your circle to follow suit. Boundaries are fences that guard the delicate flower of healing, and permit your healing to flourish in a safe environment.

A Network for Every Season

As the landscape changes constantly in healing, your network of support will be your constant. It's there to celebrate your triumphs, support you when you are in a dark moment and to remind you of your inherent ability to overcome any challenges. As a tree's roots hold it together during hurricanes, your network of support helps you stay afloat during the turbulent times of life.

Be aware that the path to recovery isn't linear. Your network of support can be a source of security and confidence regardless of when the road is uncertain. Through nurturing your community, you create an environment of love and care, a space that you feel loved by others, felt heard, and loved as the wonderful person that you are.

Chapter 20: Holistic Approaches To Healing

A more heightened awareness of the self you are in could lead to a calmer living style, and eventually allow you to recognize the appearance of PTSD signs. The research suggests that engaging in practices such as the practice of meditation, hypnotherapy and visualization and acupuncture in addition, could provide significant benefits in treating PTSD.

4.1 Exploring Inner Landscapes for Complex PTSD Recover

When it comes to the field of trauma healing in the field of trauma recovery, mindfulness and meditation serve as the foundation of healing providing a refuge in the turbulent surges of complicated posttraumatic stress. While we are on this transformational journey and begin cultivating an intimate relationship with the current moment. A relationship that firmly cradles our personal experiences in a an unprejudiced awareness.

The Dance of Awareness: Embracing the Present Moment

Think of your mind as an expansive wide, uncluttered field where emotions, thoughts and feelings whirl like leaves carried by wind. It is a way to become the spectator of this twirling dance as you observe its change in the flow and not get caught in its motions. When you are grounded in the present moment by focusing on the present moment, you can create space for exploring your own inner world through an open mind and selflove.

The Sanctuary of the Breath: An Anchor in Turbulent Waters

Pay attention to your breath as a permanent anchor to bind your body to the moment. Begin to feel the rise and fall of your chest, and the breath's rhythm, the exhalation and inhalation. Every breath you take it is a gentle way to shift your mind away from thoughts of the past and concerns about the future. As you breathe there is a place in which you can relax in peace, meditate, and then return to the center of your being.

LovingKindness Meditation: Nourishing the Soil of SelfCompassion

Complex PTSD can leave marks in the selfesteem, selfesteem. Begin with lovingkindness meditation. It is an exercise in cultivating unending compassion towards oneself as well as other people. Begin by sending kind thoughts to yourself. Saying things such as "May I be safe, may I be happy, may I be healthy, may I live with ease." When these thoughts are a part of your life and you nourish the earth of selfcompassion. Allow it to blossom with every repeated affirmation.

Body Scan: Connecting to the wisdom of the Body

The body is the repository for the fingerprints of our lives, quietly watching our sufferings as well as victories. Take a body scan, a slow journey through the world of feelings. Begin with your feet as you move up, paying attention to every sensation with a gentle interest. While you listen to the bodily's screams, you begin to establish a deep connection, a dialog between your consciousness and the inner wisdom in your body.

Inculcating resilience through Mindful Moving

The movement of the body is a pathway to healing and healing. It is an avenue that connects the body and mind into the most graceful way. Take part in mindful movements such as yoga that is gentle or taichi. Be aware of the stretching of your muscles and the flow of your breath and the cadence of your heartbeat. Each time you move with intention it honors your body's resilience and a calming harmony of renewal.

When we practice meditation and mindfulness it is possible to discover how to be present, an art that allows us to tackle the challenges of PTSD by embracing grace and strength. While you are in this journey, keep in mind that every minute is an opportunity for healing. as well as a canvas on which to can paint your personal recovery work.

4.2: Yoga for Trauma Recovery

The incorporation of yoga into your trauma rehabilitation journey is transformational and inspiring. As trauma is a part of your body, it will the healing process be a part of it. Yoga provides a unique method to gently reconnect to your body, fostering selfawareness and increasing resilient. This article will walk you through the fundamentals and techniques of yoga to aid in rehabilitation from trauma.

The Wisdom of Embodiment

Trauma can lead to disconnect with our bodies in order to shield us from intense sensations. Yoga as a practice, by its very nature is a deep connection with our body. Through mindfully executing asanas (poses) and focusing on mindful breathing, you can create an environment that allows you to experience the body's sensations, feelings and experiences that might have been buried. In this way, you are forming the base of your healing process.

Integrating Breath and Movement

The practice of mindful breathing, known as pranayama is an essential part of yoga that is traumainformed. Breath awareness helps you control your nervous system, giving you a sense of security and tranquility. Breathing in conjunction with movements during yoga will not only increase your physical agility and strength, it assists in the release of tension stored in the body. It will be explored through techniques to encourage an exploration of the physical capabilities, while recognizing your limitations.

Creating Safety on the Mat

Traumasensitive yoga is based on choices, control as well as comfort. I'll assist you in creating an environment of safety to practice in one in which you are able to pay attention to the body's signals and choose your postures that are in alignment with your personal needs. The class will explore variations and modifications of postures, making sure that you are able to achieve your personal style and still feel a sense security and confidence.

Grounding and Centering

Grounding exercises are crucial for trauma healing. With specific yoga postures and meditation techniques that will help you remain to the present and create a sense security. This is particularly beneficial in times of anxiety and stress helping you to return to a balance and the ability to control.

SelfCompassion and Mindfulness

Yoga can be a way to show yourself kindness and to cultivate selfcompassion. The practice of mindfulness, which is a fundamental part of the practice of yoga, allows you to look at your thoughts and emotions without judgment. Through incorporating mindfulness in your yoga practices it will help you develop abilities that go beyond your mat that allow you to manage emotional triggers more mindfully and with greater ease.

Building resilience through Progression

The journey of yoga will be a gradual way that builds endurance. You'll be able to progress through a sequence of yoga practices to meet the changing needs of your body. As you progress into the next stage, you'll begin to engage in postures that previously have been unattainable and will reflect the improvement that you've made in your journey to healing.

Be aware that every person's healing process is different for each person. This section is to offer strategies and information that are rooted in traumainformed yoga supported with the guidance of embodied awareness and selfcompassion. While you are embarking on this journey of transformation, give you the space to adjust to, alter, and respect your body's wisdom at every step of your way. By practicing yoga, you will discover the profound link between breath, movement and healing. You'll be able to progress towards gaining control of your emotions and enhancing your overall wellbeing.

4.3 Explore Healing Through Expressionist Arts Therapies

The world is changing of expressive arts therapies, a world in which creativity can be a channel to healing and selfdiscovery. In this segment we'll look at the ways that the various artistic forms helps to facilitate emotional release as well as selfexpression. It can also help to connect to oneself. As I've observed through my work with patients and in my clinical practice, you will also discover that these treatments provide a distinct method of dealing with the trauma of your life and fostering your natural resilient.

Embracing the Language of Art

Drawing, painting and sculpting, dance, and writing these are the expressions that connect the soul and heart. Therapies that express the arts provide an environment in which words may fail in allowing you to convey complicated emotions that otherwise be buried in. With these techniques they will take you on an exploration of your own self and uncovering the parts of yourself that need to be acknowledged and seen.

The Healing Power of Creativity

The art of creating isn't about producing the perfect masterpiece. It's about accepting your true self. When you take part in creative expression, you are tapping into your inner self and invite those aspects that are not spoken about in your past trauma to be revealed. When you're squeezing color on the canvas or writing poetry, your work reflect your feelings and the memories. While you're in the method, you'll discover that creating is therapeutic in its own right.

Chapter 21: Reclaiming Emotional Control

Hello, fellow travellers who are on the road to healing. When we begin this section, "Reclaiming Emotional Control," we dive deep into the core of dealing with the turbulent seas associated with Complex PTSD. Through compassionate advice and the wisdom that comes from holistic techniques We'll embark on an adventure to gain control in the turbulent waves of emotion that frequently occur in the aftermath of trauma.

Within the calming warmth of these pages, we'll discuss profound ideas and tools that can assist you to restore an equilibrium and a sense of empowerment. Like a skilled seaman discovers how to harness wind's power, you too can draw the energy of your own by navigating through storms, emotional triggers and adversity in a graceful and resilient manner.

Let us discover together the art of understanding the signs, recognizing, and managing emotions. While we travel towards the future, you will discover how transformative it is to gain the control of your emotions. This is a gift that you can give yourself and an affirmation to your unwavering determination.

5.1: Understanding Emotional Triggers

These triggers can be compared to keys that open the doors to past events that trigger powerful physiological and emotional responses that are confusing and disorienting. In this segment we'll look at the complex network of triggers as well as their profound impact over those who have recovered of Complex PTSD.

Navigating the Trigger Landscape

Triggers aren't just a nuisance and are actually signs pointing our way to unresolved traumas. Similar to a compass that guides the lost and triggers offer vital details regarding the unresolved aspects of our past trauma. If we understand their source and effects, we are able to change triggers into opportunities to development.

The Ripple Effect of Trauma

The effects of trauma ripple through our lives leaving imprints behind that echo throughout the course of time. The emotional triggers are often triggered by the echos that remind us of times when we were feeling helpless, afraid or even abandoned. The body can recall what our minds forgets and triggers may create a flurry of feelings that take us back to those traumatic times.

Recognizing the Warning Signs

Recognizing triggers can be an essential skill to have on your way to a successful recovery. Increased anxiety, a faster heart rate or an unanticipated increase in anger physical reactions are similar to alarm signals. Through cultivating awareness and mindfulness We can recognize the signals prior to them escalating and allow us to react instead of reacting.

Unearthing the Roots of Triggers

The process of looking back into the past may be a daunting task, but it's a crucial method of discovering triggers. They are usually connected to certain situations or interactions that have shaped our perception of the world. When we dig up the roots of these triggers uncovering the tales that still influence our current emotional environment.

Embracing Compassion and Curiosity

The notion of judgment is unsuitable within the world of triggers. Instead, we need to confront our triggers with kindness and an open mind. If we are able to become allies with ourselves, we provide an environment that is safe to investigate the root causes of the vulnerability.

The Power of Integration is Reclaiming the Power

The goal of learning about triggers is the integration. Through identifying, examining the root injuries they expose and rewriting our story about trauma. Integration helps us regain emotional control and creates a more intimate connection to our self and our present.

Keep in mind, dear reader in your game of triggers, it is not on your own. As a group, we begin a an adventure of delving into the past, accepting the present, and then reclaiming the future. When you look through the subsequent pages will you discover the methods and strategies to change triggers that are adversaries to allies.

5.2: Coping Strategies for Emotional Regulation

We welcome you to the experience of mastering the art of emotional regulation. In this chapter we explore the best techniques for coping that allow the user to take back control of his emotions in the tangled terrain that is Complex PTSD. Through honed techniques will help you discover the ability to find equilibrium amid the emotional chaos.

1. The Sanctuary of Breath

Visualize that your breathing is a trusted guide through the turbulent waters of emotion. Begin by paying attention to the beat of your breathing. Take a deep breath, allowing your stomach to expand when you expand your airways. Breathe slowly, and release all tension. Breathing with awareness keeps you in the present moment, assisting to ease the pressure of intense emotions.

2. Embrace Grounding Techniques

The ability to ground is a crucial element of your emotional regulation toolkit. Make use of your senses in order to tie you to your current situation. Choose five objects you feel, four objects that you can feel and feel, three objects you are able to listen to, two things you are able to smell and one you could feel. The simple task will distract you from negative emotions, and connects the world around you.

3. Mindful Observation

Engage in mindful observation and becoming an unprejudiced observer of your thoughts and feelings. Visualize them as clouds moving over the skies of your mind. Be aware of their form, color and intensity while not relating to their stories. This helps to break away from the story which allows you to respond to feelings with a sense of discernment, instead of reactivity.

4. Engage the Power of SelfCompassion

Give the same love for yourself as you give a friend you love. If you feel emotions are raging, accept your feelings without judgement. Imagine yourself being a comforter to yourself in the same way you could comfort a grieving child. Selfcompassion is a nurturing lotion, easing the pain of traumas past and allowing the space to heal.

5. Create an Emotional Toolkit

Create a customized toolkit of actions that improve your emotional health. Take part in activities that provide happiness, like music, art, or walks in nature. These actions will provide you with a sense of security from emotional distress and help the person to change their focus away from stress to resilience.

6. Nurture Inner Dialogue

Create an internal dialogue, with selflove and assurance. As emotions get more intense, you can offer yourself calming phrases like "This too shall pass," "I am stronger than I know," or "I am safe in this moment." The internal story becomes your sanctuary and helps to ward off the grip of emotional distress.

7. Progressive Muscle Relaxation

Tension can be found within the body, along with emotional stress. You can engage in progressive relaxation by tightening your muscles and then relaxing muscles. Begin with your feet and gradually work your way toward your head. The practice is not just good for physical relaxation, it can also lead into mental relaxation.

Keep in mind that the path to emotional control is a process rather than a goal. Take these steps with patience and determination. Once you implement them in your routine and experience the transformation of chaos in your emotions into an enchanting symphony of selfmastery. The ability you have is there to maneuver through the expansive terrain of your feelings and become the director of your experience.

5.3: Practicing Grounding Techniques

When you are experiencing overwhelming emotions or suffering, the techniques of grounding provide a solid anchor for the present. The techniques will help you get back a sense and control. This allows you to reconnect with your present and the present. The practice of grounding is a crucial tool for healing of Complex PTSD. We'll look at a few effective strategies for grounding you implement into your everyday routine.

1. Five Senses Exercise

Engaging all five senses can be a powerful technique to bring your mind back to your moment. Pick a spot that is comfortable where you can sit or stand take a few slow breaths. The first step is to identify:

Five things to be able to see: Go at your surroundings and identify five things within your surroundings.

Four objects you are able to reach out to feel four different textures. choosing to concentrate on the feel of your fingers.

Three sounds you'll hear: Pay attention to the sound around you and listen to three distinct noises.

You can smell two things: sense: Take note of two distinct scents such as the smell of nature, food or even a scent that you like.

One thing that you could experience: If it is possible try a tiny taste of something to fully enjoy the flavor.

When you engage your senses you turn your focus away from negative emotions and thoughts by focusing on the now.

2. Inhalation and grounding

Your breath can be a steady support that helps you through difficult moments. Choose a peaceful place where you can lie or sit. Relax your eyes and breathe slowly, deeply. While you breathe, visualize breaths that bring you a sense tranquility and peace. When you exhale, imagine relaxing tension and worries. Concentrate your attention on the movement and rise of your chest, or the experience of your breath coming into out of your nostrils. When your mind begins wandering, gently keep your mind on the breath. This easy, yet effective technique helps reduce anxiety and help bring you back to centering.

Chapter 22: Addressing Trauma Related Flashbacks And Nightmares

We welcome you to this chapter devoted to understanding and navigating the difficult field of traumarelated flashbacks, as well as nightmares. Being survivors of Complex PTSD, we often confront the echos of our previous events in ways that can cause a lot of anxiety. In this section we'll embark on an exploration of the traumatizing experiences we have experienced with empathy and a sense of.

Dreams and flashbacks can be like unwanted visitors from the past and bring back memories that were aweinspiringly vulnerable. They could transport us to times when we were feeling overwhelmed, helpless and in a state of being trapped. As harrowing however these experiences might be, they provide us with the chance to recover. Through examining the complex nature of the impact trauma has on our psychological state We can start to uncover the threads which link the past and the current.

In the next few pages in the coming weeks, we'll explore the scientific basis behind flashbacks and nightmares. We will shed light on what causes them and what they do to our lives. We will examine a number of strategies that can assist you in navigating these situations which will allow you to recover confidence and control. Based on traditional therapy strategies and cuttingedge techniques we'll collaborate to develop a customized toolset that will help you overcome and change the haunting echo.

Keep in mind that you're not the only one on this journey. There have been many who have gone through this journey ahead of you, and I'm there to assist you at each step of the way. Through openness, confidence, and the strategies we'll discuss in this section You're now ready to confront your flashbacks from trauma as well as nightmares with greater vigor and knowledge. Let's work together towards recovery and healing.

6.1 Identifying and Managing Flashbacks

We welcome you to the process of identifying and managing flashbacks, a vital aspect of recovering of Complex PTSD. In this segment we'll dive into the complex nature of flashbacks. We'll unravel the threads linking them to past events. This is the Dr. Arielle Schwartz, and I'm here to serve as your guide through the inner landslide together.

The Uninvited Guests: Defining Flashbacks

Flashbacks feel like visitors from our past coming into our current experience with a heightened sense of urgency. They may make us feel like we've traveled back in time and reliving traumatic experiences like they're happening in a new way. The triggering episodes can be an attempt by the mind to deal with an unresolved trauma. Often, they stem in the aftermath of events that were for the mind to handle when they occurred.

Recognizing the Signs: Identifying Flashbacks

Recognizing flashbacks is the initial way to master these. They may manifest in a variety of manners: physically, emotionally, as well as cognitively. The signs of emotional distress could include abrupt surges of anxiety, fear or panic. Likewise, physical indicators could include a racing heart, slow breathing or trembling. You may notice your mind racing or feel detached from your surroundings.

The Grounding Techniques of Tapping Moving Back to the Present

If a flashback begins to take hold the grounding methods become valuable instruments. They serve as anchors which allow you to change your attention on the present, away from the traumatic past and into the more secure present. In this course, we will explore mindfulness methods such as sensory awareness, and breathing. Engaging your senses, and reconnecting your body, you will be able to make a connection back to the present.

The Gentle Art of SelfCompassion: Easing the Impact

When we collaborate to deal with flashbacks, let me encourage that you develop selfcompassion. Keep in mind that you're not limited by the trauma you have experienced or flashbacks. Give yourself a dose of kindness and understanding while you travel this difficult landscape. It's an act of courage to address these inner echos by addressing them, and when you do so you're taking important actions towards your recovery.

Integration and Moving Forward: Progressing on Your Healing Path

Flashbacks are not just about gaining understanding how to manage the effects. They also involve connecting these episodes in your larger healing story. When we continue to move forward, we'll be able to discover the wisdom that lies within these events. As time passes, you'll realize that the wisdom of your history is able to be leveraged to push your forward in the direction of growth and resilience.

Be aware that you're not on your own in this adventure. With these exercises and words I'll be with you, helping your journey as you discover ways to get through and overcome memories. We'll work together to navigate through the turns and twists, getting stronger and closer with your true self.

6.2: Navigating Nightmares and Sleep Disturbances

We welcome you to the transformational adventure of confronting the complicated area of nightmares as well as sleep issues in the recovery process of Complex PTSD. This section will explore the intricate nature of your brain's nightly journeys. The echoes of your trauma could manifest into troubling dreams, and disturb the rest of your sleep. When we walk this journey with you, keep in mind that healing doesn't just have to be to find comfort in sunlight, but also in the peaceful sanctuary of your dreams.

Understanding the Nighttime Landscape:

As a vessel navigates unknown waters, our fantasies traverse the depths the unconscious mind. Dreams can appear when the unconscious mind process an unsolved issue, replaying parts of traumatic memories. The dreams may be intense or overwhelming and can be scary, leaving behind a puddle of intense emotion that remains when you wake up.

The SleepEmotion Connection:

The interaction between sleep and emotional state is an intricate dance. Insomnia can intensify emotional reactivity, and worsen symptoms associated with Complex PTSD. However, distress from emotional issues could affect sleep and trigger insomnia and disturbed sleep. When we unravel this complex link, we are able to bring balance back to the inner and outer worlds as well as your routines of sleep.

Embarking on the Healing Path:

1. Create a peaceful sanctuary Start by nourishing your sleeping surroundings. Make sure that the space you sleep in is peaceful, cozy and conducive to a peaceful sleep. Lights that are soft, relaxing colors as well as comfortable bedding could provide a sanctuary to rest and relax.

2. Setting up a routine for bedtime Create a relaxing bedtime routine that informs your body and your mind that it's time to relax. This might include things such as reading a soothing book, using mindfulness techniques, or engaging in a series of deep breathing exercise.

3. Involving with Nightmares: Think of dreams as messengers of the subconscious, providing important insights regarding your journey to healing. The act of writing about your dreams may offer a secure space to examine their meaning and themes. They will gradually lose the emotional restraining force.

4. Methods for Dream Reprocessing: Think about using techniques such as imagery

rehearsal therapy, in which you recreate your dreams' narrative with a method that empowers your. This technique creates an awareness of your own agency in your dreams, which allows you to make changes to the narrative of your unconscious mind.

5. Looking for professional guidance: If you are experiencing sleep problems and nightmares an experienced therapist who is trained working with trauma can provide specific treatments, like Eye Movement Desensitization and Reprocessing (EMDR) and could target the cause of the issue and help facilitate healing at a fundamental degree.

Keep in mind that the road towards healing the nighttime traumas isn't an easy one. Take your time and be mindful of each step to cultivate a peaceful sleeping. Consider your night as a canvas on which you will paint your story through resilience. Gradually, you will transform it into a place that is healing and rejuvenation. When you traverse this dark and bleak landscape be aware that you have the ability to conquer your sleep and wake up to more peaceful, brighter mornings.

6.3: Integrating Traumatic Memories

The long and arduous process of healing through Complex PTSD, the process of processing traumatic events is thought to stand as a crucial crossroad which calls us to courageously confront our past, in order to create a safe and a healthy environment inside us. This complex dance of acknowledging the suffering of our past and ensuring the present wellbeing demands a softer, but determined, method. When we enter the process of integrating painful memories, we begin journey of change that is guided by selfawareness, compassion and the art of mindfulness.

The Tapestry of Traumatic Memories

The memories of trauma are often in a splinter, and are woven into the fabric of our mind. They are echoes of the past, and influence our thoughts, emotions, and behavior in ways which we aren't able to fully appreciate. The process of integrating these memories resembles to securing an eagle through the web of our life, weaving the threads that are scattered into one cohesive whole. When we do this we acknowledge and respect the intelligence of our brainbody system which has defended us from harm, even when that required partitioning difficult events.

Cultivating Presence and Safety

The most important aspect to memory integration lies the development consciousness in the present, a fundamental element in healing. Through fostering a sense confidence within ourselves, it is possible to build a safe space in which these memories will be able to emerge into our awareness. Through mindfulness, we can become a beacon of light for us, and allows us to observe with a gentle touch the thoughts and feelings while not being caught up with them. By focusing on selfcompassion and selfcompassion, we can create a space that allows the relics from our past be redeemed.

The Dance of Resourcing and Processing

Memory integration involves a complex process which combines processing and resourcing. When we participate in this dance of a lifetime it is possible to recognize the external and internal resources that provide us with the strength we need. These are our ally to help us explore the depths of memory processing. Through the insight of a loving witness we can navigate through the complexities of our lives, processing memories with renewed power.

Honoring the Unfolding Narrative

Every memory has its own story, an element of our own personal story that is longing to be recognised. The process of integration invites us to treat these stories by observing them with awe and curiosity as we embrace the complex feelings they can bring. In allowing these stories to breathe and breathe, we give us the chance to change the way they impact our present life. Through this process of reclamation it is possible to let go of the sway of our past and gain the power to shape our lives.

Embracing the Unfoldment

When we explore the area of integration into memory and integration, we begin an enlightening journey of selfdiscovery. The journey isn't linear but rather an unfolding procedure that takes patience and selfcare. As a flower grows petals by petals and our past experiences unfold in their own time. As we go through this holy process we are both gardener and gardener caring for the soil within our bodies with love and tenderness.